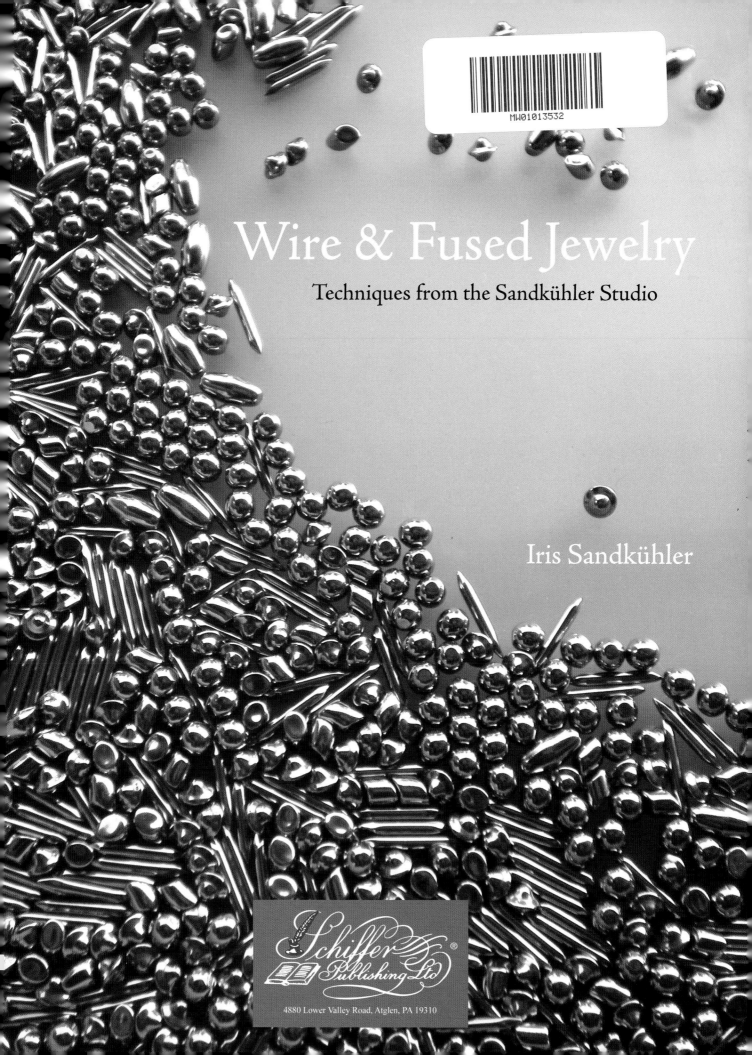

Wire & Fused Jewelry

Techniques from the Sandkühler Studio

Iris Sandkühler

Schiffer Publishing Ltd

4880 Lower Valley Road, Atglen, PA 19310

Copyright © 2010 by Iris Sandkühler

All photographs taken by Iris Sandkühler unless otherwise stated.

Library of Congress Control Number: 2009943945

All rights reserved. No part of this work may be reproduced or used in any form or by any means—graphic, electronic, or mechanical, including photocopying or information storage and retrieval systems—without written permission from the publisher.

The scanning, uploading and distribution of this book or any part thereof via the Internet or via any other means without the permission of the publisher is illegal and punishable by law. Please purchase only authorized editions and do not participate in or encourage the electronic piracy of copyrighted materials.

"Schiffer," "Schiffer Publishing Ltd. & Design," and the "Design of pen and inkwell" are registered trademarks of Schiffer Publishing Ltd.

Designed by John P. Cheek
Cover design by Bruce Waters
Type set in Adobe Jenson Pro/Zurich BT

ISBN: 978-0-7643-3445-0
Printed in China

Schiffer Books are available at special discounts for bulk purchases for sales promotions or premiums. Special editions, including personalized covers, corporate imprints, and excerpts can be created in large quantities for special needs. For more information contact the publisher:

Published by Schiffer Publishing Ltd.
4880 Lower Valley Road
Atglen, PA 19310
Phone: (610) 593-1777; Fax: (610) 593-2002
E-mail: Info@schifferbooks.com

For the largest selection of fine reference books on this and related subjects, please visit our web site at
www.schifferbooks.com
We are always looking for people to write books on new and related subjects. If you have an idea for a book please contact us at the above address.

This book may be purchased from the publisher.
Include $5.00 for shipping.
Please try your bookstore first.
You may write for a free catalog.

In Europe, Schiffer books are distributed by
Bushwood Books
6 Marksbury Ave.
Kew Gardens
Surrey TW9 4JF England
Phone: 44 (0) 20 8392 8585; Fax: 44 (0) 20 8392 9876
E-mail: info@bushwoodbooks.co.uk
Website: www.bushwoodbooks.co.uk

Dedication

It's obvious that none of us would be here if it weren't for our mother. I owe every creative instinct and act to my mother, Ursula Sandkühler Cato, who has supported my endeavors since the first day that I was able to play. I'm grateful that she's able to witness the fruits of her labor evolve into what she hoped for.

This oil portrait of my mother was painted in 1960 by my grandfather, Jupp Tietz. He made a living as a painter and muralist in Germany.

9780764334450

Preface

I have been writing since I was a child. The first journals were too embarrassing to go back and read, so at the age of twelve, I buried them somewhere in the sandy pine forests of Coastal North Carolina. Afterward I regretted it and swore that, no matter what, I would never destroy another journal. As I write this, I am in my fifties and have a closet stuffed full of them. They have evolved from pen and paper into a combination of "dear diary," scrap books, artist books, photo albums, floppy disks, zip drives, memory sticks, CDs, and flash drives.

This book is a culmination of my life and professional experience. It is a combination of how I talk to my adult students in the classroom, the influence of technical writing "day jobs," and the written voice of my journals. Rather than a dry how-to instruction manual, this is more of a "fine arts jeweler" slice of life that I am eager to share with you. I believe that being a good teacher includes being a good storyteller, especially when it comes to explaining challenging topics and putting things into context. When we understand why things are done in a particular way, it gives insight into how to branch out on a unique creative path. It also hones trouble-shooting skills.

The first half of this book is a detailed discussion of the tools and materials used in my projects. More than shopping advice, I cover a host of topics gleaned from personal experience. In other words, I've gone through a lot of trial and error so you don't have to! Whether you are new to metalsmithing or returning for the intermediate to advanced projects, please read the entire book before starting; the tools, materials, techniques, and concepts build on each other. There are many roads to enlightenment! I may be using different methods than the ones you have learned and a lot of your questions will be answered before asked.

This book takes my skills and anecdotes – from my university classrooms to my experiences as a student, professor, and distance-learning instructor – and launches them across time and space. Through this venue, I look forward to visiting with my students past, present, and future. Enjoy!

Photographic self portrait of Iris Sandkühler in a grain of molten fine silver.

Contents

Acknowledgments

The other day I saw a bumper sticker on a car that said, "What are you grateful for?" None of us lives in a void. If it weren't for the influence of people throughout my life, I wouldn't be sitting here in the comfort of a Maui hotel room, starting this book while travel-teaching on the islands. I am living my dream career: being an artist, teacher, and writer. My mother always said that you need two lifetimes: the first to learn how everything works, and the second to do it. If that's true, I'm ahead of the curve.

As a young college student, it didn't occur to me to thank Professor Donald Duncan, who introduced me to the fundamentals of metalsmithing at The Ohio State University. By approving infinite amounts of independent studies, he encouraged me to strike out on my own. The result fostered an environment of inquisitiveness, research, experimentation, and creativity.

During my student days in Columbus, Ohio, I met a local artist and jeweler Ruth Markus. As our friendship evolved, she periodically gifted me with some of her jewelry-making tools and books. As I've grown older, the meaning of this simple act has blossomed within me. I have also passed on tools and books to younger students in my life, such as Shireen, who began taking private lessons at the age of ten. Recently I attempted to contact Ruth to tell her about this book and I was saddened to learn from her brother that she has Alzheimer's disease. I come away from this bit of news wishing that I had made a greater effort to keep close contact with someone who inspired me so much.

When I was a professor at Georgia Southern University, I encouraged my jewelry students to take jewelry classes and workshops elsewhere during their summer breaks. In the fall we would reconvene and teach each other new tricks. In the summer of 1996, I lived in Manhattan. While there, I took my own advice and signed up for an intensive class on Ancient and Classical Jewelry Techniques at The Jewelry Arts Institute. Today, fusing is my forte, and I'm grateful to The Jewelry Arts Institute for reviving museum-quality, handmade jewelry techniques so that I can pass this knowledge on to my students.

It's inevitable that when I am interviewed for a job or article, Christo and Jeanne-Claude's names pop up. How (interviewers ask) has working with these internationally acclaimed environmental sculptors influenced my work? It hasn't. More precisely, it has influenced my determination to "do it my way," as Frank Sinatra sang. Witnessing their struggles to achieve their artistic visions against all odds makes the logistics of what I do seem miniscule. I'm grateful to have been close enough to them to witness that anything can be accomplished with enough patience, perseverance and dedication.

If a tree fell in the woods and no one was there to hear, would it make a sound? That pretty much sums up why I'm grateful to my students! They motivate and energize me. My student audience includes those in universities, colleges, continuing education, retirement homes, retail venues, distance learning, private lessons, and travel teaching (Hawaii, Alaska, Georgia, and North Carolina). I'm grateful for returning faces and those who have chosen to invite me into their homes and social gatherings.

In my immediate life: thank you Mark Hogsett for keeping me grounded, holding down the fort, and feeding our pet menagerie when I am away travel teaching. Thanks Amy Rose, for editing. Jenny Lee, graphic designer and webmaster, who keeps www.sandkuhler.com running smoothly. Charles Walz, who helps me remain physically fit and helped edit this book. Natalee Thomas, friend and owner of Adorna Bella, for featuring my jewelry at her shop in North Beach, San Francisco. Thanks to Lillian Jones for being my professional development buddy.

Introduction

Biography of the Author

By Terry Graham
Marketing & Public Relations Consulting
Tiburon California, January 2009

Iris Sandkühler is a fine artist based in Northern California whose creative endeavors encompass a broad range of art forms including eclectic collages/montages, pen-and-ink figurative drawings, exquisitely handcrafted gold, silver, and copper jewelry, whimsical accessories, and everything in between. An exceedingly versatile talent, Iris is comfortable working with both two- and three-dimensional media.

Iris' work reflects her highly creative spirit, mastery of diverse technical skills, and love of producing art that is at once bold, organized, and often highly detailed. Since 1982, she has created a unique mix of fine art and jewelry displayed in select galleries and boutiques nationwide. Her experience, education, and training have allowed her to develop academic curricula and continuing education classes as well as hands-on workshops for individuals wishing to explore their own creativity.

Born in Germany, Sandkühler came to the United States when her mother married an American in the military. Her mother's family survived both World War I and II with few possessions other than jewelry with modest but sentimental value. These pieces had endured because jewelry was worn to bed at night along with clothing necessary to quickly flee one's home to crowded, communal bomb shelters during air raids. For Iris's mother, this jewelry represented physical links to faraway relatives and served as the centerpiece for sharing family history and anecdotes with her daughter. Stories of the origins of each piece made family members come alive, revealing artists such as Iris's grandfather, who was an oil painter and muralist, her father, a professional photographer, and both grandmother and mother, who enjoyed handicrafts such as knitting and crocheting. Sandkühler's eclectic creative interests reflect the various influences of her family.

Iris's jewelry designs range from delicate, handmade gold and silver chains to wire weaves that

Tosca (my borzoi) and I, taken after writing my first distance learning lesson in August of 2004. These lessons set the stage for writing this book. You can find out more about my distance learning program at www.sandkuhler.com

My father, Werner Sandkühler, was a professional photographer who often used the legendary Rhine River as a background. This self portrait was taken in the summer of 1957.

recycled materials, and diverse components that students use as they apply newly acquired skills.

Iris's exhibition list – including group, solo, invitational, and juried shows and trunk show appearances – is extensive. Select locations include the White House; Tokyo; New York City; San Francisco; Tiburon, California; North Carolina; Georgia; Ohio; Illinois; Alaska, and Hawaii. She also sells her creations while on the road to travel and teach.

To learn more about Iris, see her resume, read articles, view her travel-teaching schedule, calendar and window-shop for project-based workshops, visit www.sandkuhler.com.

One of the highlights of teaching for the University of Hawaii, Maui Community College in 2008 was living without electricity in a tree house, on the edge of a canyon in a jungle.

hold asymmetrical gemstones, sea glass, and found objects. An expert in metalsmithing, she is also skilled in ancient and classical techniques including fusing – an alternative to soldering that is cleaner and less toxic and permanently combines fine gold or silver pieces together.

During her years of studying and creating artwork, Iris has taught and developed curricula for academic programs. She has served as an Assistant Professor at Eastern Illinois University and Georgia Southern University and as an instructor at various community colleges, including City College of San Francisco. More recently, her distance-learning lessons, available as online courses, teach a wide range of metalsmithing skills to students around the world. Iris also teaches private lessons and onsite workshops at various locations across the country, combining her love of travel with work at destination sites.

Her studio in Marin County, California, reflects her highly organized, systematic approach to her materials – with walls and drawers containing gemstones, glass, metals, stones, bones, found objects,

Content
What Is It and Where Can I Get Some?

When you choose the objects to add to your Lucky Horseshoe Charm Bracelet, you are working with content. *Content*, or the unifying meaning behind art/jewelry objects, is a concept that is not generally discussed in jewelry *workshops*. I believe, however, that it is the most important ingredient in a mature and professional body of work, because it separates your work from everyone else's. Working with content can become a life-long endeavor influenced (or thwarted) by the educational venues that you attend. I'd like to briefly compare some of these venues: academic, private lessons, workshops and learning on your own.

The rich, manmade, saturated orange colors from plastic guppies, iridescent beads, and Swarovski crystals juxtaposed with the warm, natural hues of sea shells create a visual dialogue. The linear quality of the shells is repeated in acrylic cocktail picks. The guppies are contained in a Lady Schick (razor) container (c.1965), of the same color, which my mother recently gave me. A teal hat box lid vignettes the objects like a stage and symbolizes an ocean on a sunny day. Any physical or psychological aspect of this collection could evolve into jewelry or create a backdrop for photography.

Inspiration for materials can come from anywhere. My collections live all over the studio and home. I add to them over time as I find objects and as people give me things. A well-stocked studio is like a well stocked kitchen that is ready at any time to create something wonderful. This particular collection is about color, texture, movement, and carefree summer memories.

Academics and Fine Arts: My professional background is in visual fine arts. One of the joys of being a professor is that I have years to develop a relationship with my students. During this time, it's the student's goal to create something new to enrich their visual vocabulary as well as to enrich humanities in general. My job is to guide them in research and tapping into unique perspectives to develop content or meaning in their work.

When artists have shows, the body of work reflects a theme or preoccupation. A written artist statement is required to contextualize the work and help orient the viewer. It can also be used as a critiquing tool (for better or worse). Often, these statements are the jumping-off point for marketing: pamphlets, catalogues, articles, and books. Successful shows have the power to educate and entertain; they can be cathartic, whimsical and ultimately, they can teach us to be more human, which is why the arts are included in the humanities.

Private Lessons: Over an extended period of time, private lessons can provide a similar path to academics in professional development. I coach my private lesson students in setting research goals, identifying subject matter, working with content and increasing technical skills. On a good day, this process is insightful, rewarding, cathartic, and extremely satisfying. On a bad day, it can feel boring, challenging, frustrating, and painful. The equivalent to this level of self-discovery in academics is independent studies and graduate-level work and it's not always easy. The grading system locks in commitment and ensures that students follow through, even when the going gets tough. The down-side of private lessons is that meetings are voluntary and commitment can become fleeting, especially when life gets in the way.

Workshops: As a workshop instructor, I'm painfully aware of the limitations in time that my students face. The short (often single) sessions don't permit me to get to know my students. All the project challenges have also been smoothed over by me (the workshop instructor) to ensure that everyone works in unison to finish the project, which determines the success of a workshop. Individuals who want to forge into new creative territory and challenge themselves further have to be self motivated and disciplined to explore on their own. Sometimes they end up as (what I call) serial workshop takers.

On Your Own: Another way to find support in developing content in your work is to have a professional artist/teacher/jeweler give you a portfolio review. Sometimes joining a club or professional guild that holds critiques is beneficial. Honest feedback from peers and professionals in your field is essential for growth.

A good way to begin working on content is to carry around an artist's journal. While academics encourage large formats, I believe the book should be convenient enough in size so that you'll always have it with you. In it, you will capture enough notes, sketches or taped pieces of newspapers, magazines, etc., to record those spontaneous and sometimes fleeting moments of inspiration. The pages should be free from decorative elements from the manufacturer so as not to unduly influence or distract you. Blank or graph lines work best.

Mixing the artist's book with journaling is a great way to explore your thoughts and observations. Look for repetitive preoccupations, especially with color, shapes, or emotions. What is it that you want to express? Use a lot of adjectives. What is your personal iconography? Do you have an avatar? How can you visually communicate your recurring themes in a consistent way? Will your audience see what you intended? Now, the ultimate challenge: Show us something we haven't seen before!

The Lucky Horseshoe Charm Bracelet is a great way to begin working with subject matter (what you see) and content (what it means). As a child, I watched the film *To Kill a Mocking Bird* several times. I was intrigued by the contents of the box that was secretly hidden in a tree. Someone was adding mysterious objects to it, and when the children found it, their imaginations soared with implications. As a fine artist, I have clear mason-style jars stacked everywhere in my studio with collections of objects. Organized by size, color, type, material, and other

common threads, they represent the equivalent to paint on a painter's palette. Found objects often end up in my jewelry, and I invite the viewer (purchaser, wearer) to interpret the juxtapositions and meanings through their personal filters. What have you collected? What do you want to say to the world? How can you express it with this bracelet project?

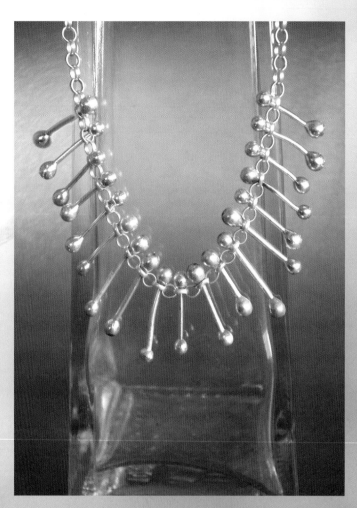

Creativity and Copyrights

When I was a fine arts professor, my students were generally graded on three things: research, technical skill, and creativity. Research was demonstrated through group presentation so my students could learn from each other. Looking at other jewelers' work and biographies, and studying culturally traditional works, gave my students and their creative endeavors context and directional leads for their own development. It also gave them a way to reference their influence rather than plagiarize.

Technical skill was learned through lectures, slide reviews, demonstrations, studio practice, and demonstrated improvement over time. Creativity was based on proposals, sketches, discussions, and plans, which were documented in their artist journals/books. These journals served as proof of development and were graded with the accompanied finished projects. Weekly critiques helped students think critically and learn to communicate. In short, the academic education gave structure and the goal was to create unique works of art, whether in drawing, sculpture, or metalsmithing.

The problem with workshops is that time is limited to a few hours compared to an academic class that covers several weeks of personal growth and development. Because workshops are confined, students aren't able to do research or indulge in guided creative exploration. Workshop instructors must organize technical skills into one bite-sized project so students are moving at the same rate with the same goal.

There is a funny movie that I saw years ago starring Michael Keaton called *Multiplicity* (1996) in which he clones himself to make his multi-faceted, hectic life easier. Initially it works, but then he begins to make more and more clones to cover more and more aspects of his life. With each new clone, the breadth of character becomes duller, watered down, single faceted and literally stupid. To make matters worse, the clones begin making their own clones. I use this scenario when talking to my students about the role of using a workshop to develop skills. It is imperative that they expand into their own uncharted creative territory rather than just making (or teaching!) the piece they learned over and over. This is how students develop their own unique line and avoid legal issues regarding intellectual property.

Unfortunately I've seen too many people take a design (or lesson) from their instructor (or magazine, book, website, etc.) and sell it as their own. How do we know this is illegal? There is always a copyright somewhere in the source. If you are making jewelry to study, own, or give as gifts, there probably won't be an issue. It's when you begin profiting (making money) off of someone else's design that you can get into trouble. To avoid litigation, do your homework. Use the techniques that you learn to develop your own original design. It is professional practice to reference your influences/teachers, but the final product shouldn't be confused with the original artist/designer's style. Document how you developed it (artist books) in case you are ever challenged. Use "engineering notebooks" as a method of doing this. Engineering notebooks are solid books that can't have pages added or torn out without it being obvious. Date your developments. In the end, if you show us something that we haven't seen before, you should be OK. If you are struggling with coming up with new ideas consider taking a university class or private lessons that focus on developing "content." Also, mix and match the techniques you've learned to create more robust pieces.

That said, if you are active in your field and knowledgeable about trends, you might notice simultaneous development. Another reason to document your creative developments is just in case you get challenged by someone somewhere else who came up with the same ideas at the same time.

For further reading on intellectual property rights and copyright issues, Google the words "jewelry" and "copyright infringement" or follow the specific cases below stemming from the fine arts and crafts fields:

- Photography and sculpture: the landmark case of Rogers v. Koons "String of Puppies."
- Regarding an original beading project: McCabe v. Eclectica Inc.
- In the field of graphic design: Shepard Fairey v. Associated Press.

TOOL TALK

How This Section is Divided

I have organized all the tools and materials, whether for hot or cold processes, in their section in alphabetical order. Please read through everything first, then go back and copy the items for your shopping list. Also review the manufacturer's guide before you begin a project (not after you've set the cat's tail on fire). I've offered lots of tidbits of information from my experience in hopes that it will make you an educated shopper when considering different brands and styles. I've also included insightful tips on how things work and why, so the project pages can focus on photos and instruction.

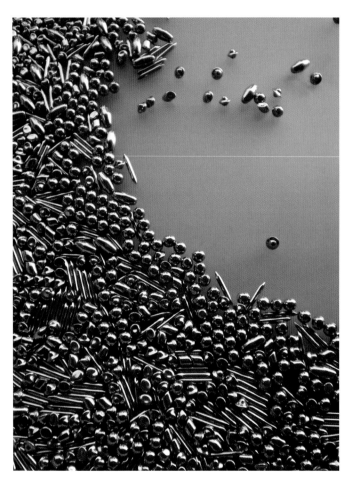

I use mixed-shape, stainless steel shot for my homemade tumbler. It's cheap, low maintenance, and low tech. The tool section has details on how to make your own.

Some tools and materials are not directly related to the projects but are generally useful. For example, a mill smooth file comes in handy if you need to remove rust from a tool or condition the edges of needle-nose chain pliers so they don't mar your fine silver project. You won't see gauge mentioned in specific projects, but you'll need one if the tag falls off your wires and you can't figure out what gauge is what.

Resources

Things change! Companies that sell jewelry tools, and materials fold, merge, buy each other out, partner up, pop up new, get outsourced, etc. Certain brands or types of tools can go out of vogue. Imported and local brands evolve and/or disappear. Since I began buying tools to haul to my classes, I've noticed that it is difficult to commit to one brand and sometimes challenging to find more of the same good tool. Quality can fluctuate when brands get outsourced or someone thinks they've improved on a tool and, in essence, created more problems. The bottom line is that sometimes a cheap tool is as good as an expensive version and expensive tools can break during the first use.

For all these reasons, I update the ever-evolving resource page on my website: www.sandkuhler.com. As I write, I am not affiliated or partnered with any of these sources in terms of getting special discounts or incentives by mentioning them. Mostly, I deal with the companies that have the best customer service and carry the items that fill the needs of my workshops and studio. I invite students to stay inquisitive and go out and try new sources. You'd be surprised at what you can find at your dentist's office, hardware – or kitchen supply store.

When I was living on the Midwest prairie and worked as an assistant professor at Eastern Illinois University, I used Rio Grande's catalogues to order what I was unable to find locally. As a small-metals professor at Georgia Southern University, I began using Rio's catalogues as a required textbook. Students only needed to call them, mention that they were a student, and set up an account to receive free catalogs. I did not require them to order from Rio, instead I suggested they use the source as a jumping-off point to begin comparison shopping. Learning to navigate through thousands of tools without getting overwhelmed is also an education in itself! Over the decades, Rio Grande's catalogs have evolved into quite the learning tool. Charts, full-color photographs, and educational blurbs give insight into usage and spur the imagination.

As I began developing my distance-learning lessons, I also required my foreign students to order Rio Grande's catalogs as textbook supplements. The catalogs "put us on the same page" in terms of which tools I was referring to.

In this book, I've listed (and written about) tools and materials alphabetically. My personal tools served as photographic models, complete with their historical nicks and scratches. Good tools become intimate companions and, like old friends, there is comfort in witnessing time and experience in their face.

Types and Brands of Tools

When shopping for tools, you often have a choice between steel and stainless steel. In general, steel is stronger and more precise in its construction. Unfortunately steel rusts and rust can transfer to your work. Stainless steel doesn't rust, but gets dinged up, and out of true (torque) faster. Which one should you purchase? It depends on the climate that you live in. In dry desert air, rust isn't an issue. But if you live in a place with humidity (the only thing worse is salty ocean air) and unless you want to spend your life reconditioning tools, I recommend you buy stainless steel. If you don't have the choice and you purchase steel, keep your tool oiled and in a container to lesson exposure to humidity when not in use.

Some manufacturers put a dark matte finish on tools to decrease reflective light that causes glare and eye strain. Great idea, unless you like working outside: I've gotten burnt picking up my tools in the sun.

At the time of this writing, I gravitate more toward the quality of tools manufactured in Germany and Switzerland. But as I mentioned earlier, things change! Look for reviews from friends, professionals, and on the web. When I talk to store clerks, I keep in mind that they are there to sell their products. I try and gain insight by asking a typical job-interview-type question with a (tool) twist: "Name one thing that you don't like about this tool."

I tend to shy away from additional gadgets that are often added to tools to improve them. I particularly dislike parts that shift out of place, fall off, or break over time. That said, there is a balance, and I also enjoy buying and trying new tools. Happy retail therapy!

Butane Torch
(Or Bringing Out the Pyro in You)

I like to joke in my classes that these torches come in two sexes. If you buy it at a kitchen store it's a crème brûlée torch. If you buy the same thing at a hardware or jewelry supply store, we call it a (I put on my manly voice) butane torch. My safety talk about torches and fire begins with a candle, then a Bic disposable lighter. Next I demonstrate pencil torches, then graduate up in tank capacity (size). One of the purposes of my talk is to show how they all work pretty much the same. I have a lot of students who are afraid of torches and fire. By deconstructing how the torches work and bluntly discussing things that could (and have) gone wrong with them, my students usually graduate from fear to healthy respect.

Each time I develop a new distance-learning lesson that involves torches, I have to retake a photo of my torch lineup. The brand names, models, shapes, etc., keep evolving, but again they all have similar things in common. Students ask which torch is my favorite. It depends on what I'm working on. In general, I tend to trust and promote metal torches more than plastic, but that's probably more of a political (environmental) statement than a safety issue. The following is a general overview of the torch anatomy starting from the bottom.

Valve

Whether it's a pencil torch or the stand-up version with the removable foot, the female valve on the bottom of the torch is compatible with the male valve on a can of butane gas. Like the leaded and unleaded dispensers at a gas station, they have a compatible mate so you don't accidentally put propane or MAPP gas in by accident. In terms of safety, I tell my students that, rather than worry about whether or not the valve is leaking, I just assume it always is and strategize from there. (I'm also the type of person that rechecks the door several times to see if it's really locked.) That being the case, you'll want to store it someplace where there isn't anything electric going on. Keep in mind that where there is an on/off switch, there's an electric spark. Find a well-ventilated space so the gas doesn't accumulate. What's worse than the torch (or butane gas can) exploding? Having it explode under the kitchen sink, taking the Drano®, Windex®, Clorox®, and rat poison with it. Or, having it go off in the closet by the front door with clothing and ski poles while you are trying to get out of your home that's on fire or trembling from an earthquake. In short, if you follow the worst-case scenario and think critically, you should be able to find a safe spot via process of elimination. It's also imperative that you read the warnings on the packaging of both the torch and the can of butane. It has helpful hints such as not to expose it to 120 degrees Fahrenheit, which pretty much negates using the trunk of your car as a storage space. Because things change, I re-read the labels with each new torch and can of butane that I purchase and recommend you do as well.

Removable Foot

Not sure why the foot needs to be removable (as opposed to being a part of the tank design), but it seems that all the stand-up butane torches have one. If I were the king, I would make it impossible to put the foot on backwards. When the foot is on properly, the torch stands like the letter "C" in profile. Improperly, it looks more like a "Z' and wants to fall forward onto the potentially hot tip, branding anything it contacts. The bigger the hole in the foot, the faster the gas can dissipate. If the gas is trapped in the foot, it can waft

up when you light the torch. Kaboom. Nice way to remove the tiny hairs on your hand.

Tank (Body)

The bigger the tank (body), the more powerful the torch. Factoring in whether it's full (more powerful) or low (less powerful). You can use this as a strategy for working on projects of different mass. For example, if you have a small torch and you need more power, fill it up. (Don't forget to let it sit at least three minutes before striking, so you don't find yourself holding a little blue ball of flame. Again, read the directions.) If your have a large torch but are working on a small project, use your torch when there is less gas in it. What's kind of cool (literally) about a metal torch is that you can feel the cold butane rise as you fill it with gas.

Striker and Regulator

I introduce my torch talk using a simple candle. The flame is soft, without a sharp, focused blue cone inside. A disposable butane lighter has a slightly bigger flame, but it is still soft and similar to a candle flame. When you compare the disposable lighter to a butane torch, they both use butane, but the torch has a hotter, more distinctly focused flame. What's the difference if they are both using the same gas? Even a pencil torch with a similar tank size to a disposable lighter is much, much hotter. The difference is the regulator. It mixes air from the room with the gas and, combined with the size/shape of the nozzle, creates more pressure. More pressure equals more heat.

Some torches have to be lit from a source. I prefer the ones that have their own built-in striker so I don't have to turn it on and fiddle with a match while the gas is coming out. It's less complicated and just feels safer.

Safety Switch

This might be the place where manufacturers express their creativity the most. I understand why the safety is there, but at times I feel like I need multiple hands to hold on to the torch, undo the safety, click the trigger, and lock the flame into place. My best advice is to keep the torch on the table as you work through your own unique set of instructions. That way you won't torch your lap or table when you figure it out. Kidding aside, I do require my students to keep the torch on the table as they are going through the safety sequence. I also require my students to turn off the torch if their hand isn't actually on it. That way if the table gets bumped, you won't set the carpet or cat on fire.

Trigger Finger (Worry Not)

Unfortunately, my favorite torch (OK, I do have a favorite after all) is the most difficult to trigger. I actually have to start squeezing the trigger with one hand then use my other to help finish squeezing the trigger. Then, while holding the trigger down, I have to lock it on. If the gas didn't ignite, I have to start the sequence over. Wow. Talk about a safety feature. It's impossible to accidentally start this puppy. Forget children, unless they are rock climbers, most of my adult students can't start the trigger. The reason I still use this torch is because of the compact body with a strong, lean, sharply focused flame. The newer model has been designed to be a little easier to trigger, but it doesn't have the punch that the old version does in terms of power. Just remember, if you trigger your torch and it doesn't ignite, there is probably still gas coming out, so you still have to turn it off.

Flame Lock

To prevent hand fatigue (cramps, shoulder aches, etc.) all my butane torch models have a flame lock. Otherwise, if you let go of the trigger, the flame goes out. You'll have to hunt for the flame lock; different brands put it in different places along the tank (pencil torches) or head (stand up torches). The flame lock is often the way to turn off the torch; that, or triggering it again.

Crank Up the Volume

Somewhere on the torch there is either a wheel or slider that allows you to turn the gas up or down. Look for a plus- and-minus symbol or an elongated triangle that represents small to large. Note that when the tank is full, you won't see much difference in the amount of flame. Conversely, when your flame starts dying because you've used up the gas, you'll get a little more mileage out of it by turning it all the way up. How do you know when the torch needs gas? When the flame is dying, turning it up no longer makes a difference, or you find yourself so close to the piece, you're about to knock it over with the torch head.

Torch Head

If your flame is fuzzy and you can't visually locate the tip of the bright blue cone (which is the part of the flame that you work with), then you may have to use the regulator to adjust the ratio of air to butane. Some models have a ring (valve) on the nozzle, containing a hole. When you turn it and line it up with another hole (under the ring), then the regulator will be able to pull in air, mix it with the gas, and create the maximum focus and heat. If the holes are not lined up, air will not be drawn in and you'll have a large, pure butane, unfocused flame.

Not all models have this ring valve on the nozzle. Some have a slider that only serves for cutting off the air flow. When I demonstrate this in class, I joke and call it the handy cigar lighter. Watch your eyebrows.

Safety in the Studio

My torch education developed via different types of jewelry studios, glass blowing- and welding shops. Some were outfitted with pony tanks of gas; others with larger, standard tanks and direct lines in. Gases included acetylene, oxy-acetylene, propane, natural, and MAPP gas. As a jewelry professor at Georgia Southern University, we used acetylene. When I decided to make the San Francisco Bay Area my home, I began teaching jewelry workshops at the local continuing education programs. The problem was that I could only teach cold jewelry classes because of limitations with the traditional jeweler's torches. One day, in 2000, I was browsing in a kitchen store in Berkeley when I spotted a crème brûlée torch. I remember standing there wondering if it got hot enough to melt silver. Deciding to give it a try, I took it home and discovered that it worked just fine for projects up to the size of a quarter or half dollar in mass. At that point, I began developing my hot jewelry workshop curriculum. The concept became popular because it was convenient and manageable for folks who didn't have the opportunity to create or go to a jewelry studio. Today everyone is doing it. Since 2000, I have bought several dozen torches, since they get heavily used and worn out in my workshops.

Crème brûlée torches sound cute, but they can be formidable when things go wrong. Here's some of the drama I've witnessed personally and as an instructor.

- Spewing wet gas across the classroom. The regulator obviously wasn't regulating.
- Unpredictable sparking flames. Could be because I stored them in a well-ventilated garage on sandy cliffs by the brutal winter Pacific Ocean.
- Torch doesn't turn off. Since blowing out the flame wouldn't stop the gas from continuing to come out, I found an open cement pad and camped out while it burned itself out.
- My favorite: sweet crème brûlée torch becomes six-foot flame thrower. This is why I talk so much about the flame overshooting the project (and potentially hitting the cookie sheet, table or student directly across). Besides being a flaw in design, this can happen because the gas has been topped off too much.
- Result of ignoring the three-minute rule about letting gas settle after filling up the torch: singed finger hairs and no need for more coffee the rest of the day.

If anything happens to the torch while you're using it, resist the urge to scream and throw it somewhere. Just turn it off and set it down as quickly and safely as possible. I speak, not just as a Leo (fire sign), but also from experience. I've gotten burnt (by myself and from being in the path of others), had my hair ignite, set the scarf wrapped around my own neck on fire (but hey, I looked quite fashionable for a while), been in both a large and small gas explosion (picture a crispy cartoon critter standing there frozen in disbelief, holding a smoldering match). Oh yes, what about those imitation long nails I tried to maintain as a jewelry student, no matter what! Well, after I set the index fingernail on fire and felt the heat transfer to my bones even after I blew it out. . . . I decided to get with the program and dress appropriately.

Should I be confessing all this? Now that it's thirty years since most of this happened (think college student), I'm happy to say it's made me so hyper-vigilant that my Atlanta friends dubbed me "OSHA Iris." In fact, it has become part of my teaching philosophy. I remind my students to always assume the worst when setting up their work station or rearranging the classroom chairs. Everything flammable (and melt-able) has to go under the table or be hung up away from any potential flame-throwing arena. Safety glasses on, hair back, natural fiber clothing (better to have them go up in flame then melt into your skin), and torch off when your hand isn't on it.

Finally, be sure to hold on to that receipt in case you need to return a wayward torch. Despite store policies, I will return the torch at any point that it becomes dangerous and unreliable. A simple offer to demonstrate the problem usually makes them highly cooperative. Have fun bringing out the inner pyro in you, but do so responsibly so you don't end up like toast.

Cookie Sheet
Dedicated to Jewelry Making, Not Cookie Baking

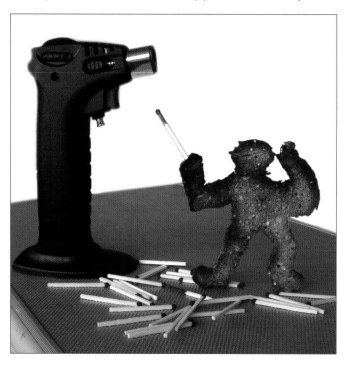

I prefer torches that are self starters, as opposed to lighting from another source, such as matchsticks. One less thing to worry about! The only duel you should engage in is with creative design, not fire safety. Be sure to read all the directions, on the torch and can of butane gas so you don't end up like toast.

What I mean by dedicated is that you make sure it isn't used in the kitchen for baking chocolate chip cookies after you've used it for jewelry projects. I recommend using a permanent marker to write JEWELRY ONLY on it so the well-meaning babysitter doesn't decide to use it.

Size Matters

The cookie sheet should be as large as you can find: at lease 19.5 X 12 inches. Size is important, because you are using it as a fire barrier. Since your torch flame can overshoot its target, the bigger the cookie sheet, the better. If in doubt, use two. In August 2006, one of my students found a full-sized aluminum cookie sheet for only five dollars, at an industrial kitchen supply place.

Coatings

Your cookie sheet should be brand new so you don't start a grease fire or contaminate your project, metals or tools. If you buy one with a Teflon coating, be sure and read the warnings. Many people don't realize that you can't use Teflon in high heat because it gets scorched and puts off an acrid toxic gas that can kill household birds. In people it is referred to as a Teflon cold, and who knows what kind of damage it can do to your health. Don't panic! Teflon cookie sheets are only meant to be a safety barrier in case of an accident. They work great as long as you don't torch them.

Shape

If you are using a cookie sheet, it should have a lip all the way around. This lip is important in case anything falls and rolls. The lip also keeps the molten metal from landing in your lap, on the floor, or boring its way to China (or to the United States if you're in China). For this reason, avoid other shapes and styles of baking pans.

Inappropriate Materials

Think critically! I've seen folks use red house bricks, stone tiles, cinder blocks, etc. What's wrong with this picture? Used by themselves, hot metal can fall in-between and onto the table. These surfaces weren't intended to be used with heat. What's worse than accidentally torching your heat shield? Torching an inappropriate brick or stone: they could could contain air pockets, or moisture, which can expand and explode.

Dowel Rods

I was first introduced to the concept of using dowel rods to measure and make consistent jump rings at The Jewelry Arts Institute in Manhattan. Each student was presented with a bundle of wooden dowels. Mine included:

- 3/4 inch
- 5/8 inch
- 1/2 inch
- 3/8 inch
- 5/16 inch
- 1/4 inch
- 3/16 inch
- 1/8 inch

More than a decade later, I still use that same bundle of wooden dowels. I've also collected some snazzy acrylic dowels from teaching on the Island of Oahu. Jason Del Mundo, co-owner of The Bead Gallery, makes and sells them. The advantage to his dowels is that wire coils come free easily. Sometimes when my students use my wooden dowels, they wind the coil too tight and they have a hard time working the coil off. At that point, I always joke that they might consider decompressing at a day spa or buying Jason's dowels.

Many places offer metal dowel rods. These can be especially handy if you need to bend a thick-gauge wire around a thin dowel. I've snapped the wood before (good reason to wear safety glasses). In a pinch, look to common items in your immediate environment such as shish kabob sticks, highlighters, pens, drinking glasses, cans, etc., to form your loops.

To make your own wooden dowels, go to any hardware store and buy one of each size. Since they are several feet long, you will have to either cut them yourself or have someone at the store do it for you. My original wooden dowels are a handy four inches. What to do with the wooden leftovers? Stake your tomatoes, give your house bunny something to chew on other than electric cords, or save them for when you make friends with other jewelers or workshop instructors!

Use a permanent marker to write the size on the ends of the dowels. For the acrylic ones, use a piece of transparent tape to write on. A ziplock bag is a great way to store your bundle. Rubber bands break as they deteriorate and the smaller dowels slip out.

File: Mill Smooth

If I were stuck on a desert island with only one file to use on my metalsmithing projects, my trusty mill smooth file would be it. I don't remember where exactly I bought mine, but I do know that it was over twenty years ago and it's still working well. Nicholson is the manufacturer.

Unless you specifically purchase a two-way file, be sure to file away from your body. One-way files only cut one direction (filing away from your body), and to drag them backwards over your work traps the filings in the teeth and closes them up. It's a good way to render your file ineffective.

When I was a professor at Georgia Southern University, one of my colleagues showed me a great trick: making a corncob handle. Not only is it a great conversation starter, it leaves your fatigued hands energized.

How to Make a Corn Cob Handle
1. After you've enjoyed your corn on the cob, take a knife and scrape it clean.
2. Break the cob in half.
3. Blot it dry with a clean rag.
4. Place somewhere to begin drying it.
5. Check on it every few hours. Rotate it until you see a split develop in the ends.
6. Push the tang (pointed handle-end of the file) into the split as far as you can.
7. Find a warm spot in your home to completely dry it. A sunny spot on a windowsill or on top of a heat register works great. Of course, don't place it anywhere that is a fire hazard.
8. The goal is to dry it faster than it has time to mold. Check on it often.
9. Don't test (pull on) the cob.

Once completely dry, the cob will have an amazing grip on the tang. Mine lasted over a decade and didn't begin coming loose until it suffered a TSA search in my airplane luggage.

Gauge
How Do You Gauge the Gauge of Your Gauge?

The word gauge can be used as a noun and a verb! A gauge is a tool used to measure the thickness of metal sheet and wire. The American B & S gauge is a round disk that has slots cut into it from the side. Whichever slot your wire sticks in is the size (gauge) of the wire. One side of the tool is marked with decimals and the other with whole numbers. In the USA we use the whole numbers. Keep this tool with you always, just in case.

Concept: The Higher the Number, the Thinner the Wire
When I was a college student, the hardest part for me to wrap my brain around was the concept that "the higher the number, the thinner the wire." Considering everything else in our world works the opposite way; bigger feet, bigger number, right? This concept would always kick in my lysdexia, I mean dyslexia.

It wasn't until I learned how to form gold wire from scratch at The Jewelry Arts Institute in Manhattan, that it all made sense to me. To create wire (and I'm simplifying here, so don't try this at home), you begin with melting down your scrap metal, hammer it into a "finger" shape and then file one end to a point. This is in preparation for pulling it through a series of graduating (in size) holes in a steel draw plate.

You begin with the largest hole that your metal finger fits in. For example: hole Size 2. After you draw the sharpened finger through hole Size 2, it gets squeezed down to that size. Next you have to anneal it to make it malleable again (heat to a dull orange glow and relax the metal, making it dead soft). Then you repeat the process (drawing down the wire and annealing it) with the next smallest hole, for example gauge Size 3.

Again and again you repeat this cycle of pulling the metal through consecutively smaller holes and annealing in-between. The numbers of the holes represent how many times (holes) you had to pull your wire through to get to the gauge you want. So by the time you get to gauge Size 16, you've gone through sixteen holes. That's why, the higher the number, the thinner the wire. Understanding the process didn't make my lysdexia go away, but it helped me visualize what was going on. Oh yes, conversely: the lower the number, the thicker the wire!

Glasses
Safety, Prescription, Readers and Magnification Visor

Protect your eyes! Please wear some type of glasses so that flying bits don't end up causing problems. Non-tinted is best so you see better and "read" the color of the metal that you are heating. I keep a collection on hand for the students who forget theirs. It includes: chemistry glasses, reading glasses, safety glasses with the side protectors, magnification visors that are worn on the head and trendy clear "fake" fashion glasses. As a professor, I also have facial shields available to those fine art students who like testing boundaries by blowing things up. (Don't try subjecting pearls to a torch flame.) To avoid headaches, I change glasses often when I'm engaged in marathon sessions of jewelry making.

Hammer
If I Had a (Good) Hammer…

As the Peter, Paul and Mary song of my youth goes: "If I had a hammer, I'd hammer in the morning, I'd hammer in the evening, all over this land." It's true! There's nothing more enjoyable (and cathartic) than whaling on a piece of metal with a great hammer (except maybe torching it). However, if I have a bad hammer, I wouldn't be hammering too long because of muscle fatigue, shoulder aches, carpal tunnel, hammer heads flying off across the room, blood blisters, hand cramps, uncontrollable missed blows; you get the picture.

My friend Lillian, whom I've known since the 1970s, is also a jewelry instructor. I gave her one of my favorite hammers as a gift. She loved it so much that she ordered a bunch for her students. It's a combination planishing (plane) and forming (form) hammer. The planishing (or flat) side, is used to flatten and stretch metal. The forming, (or round) side, is used to form or curve metal. I like to use the planishing side on wire to get it away from that "wire look" by widening it. The forming side gives it that dappled texture that shimmers in light.

What makes a hammer great?

- Balance is important. A hammer should be heavy enough to do most of the work for you, while at the same time; it should only be a small challenge to hold because of its weight.
- A hammer needs to be comfortable in your grip when held properly: at the end, not close to the head.
- Rust is bad news. If you need to clean rust off, use 3-in-1 brand household oil and steel wool (not Brillo® pads, which contain soap) to get it off. If the rust is deep, use your mill smooth file, then lightly oil the metal.
- Make sure the wooden handle smells fresh, not like mildew. Older tools might not have a coating on the wood. If you inherit such a tool, use tung oil (sounds like tongue but fear not, it has nothing to do with tongues) or wood oil to keep it from drying out.
- The head shouldn't be loose. If the head of any of my hammers get loose, I send the hammer back to the manufacturer to replace or repair. Normally, I don't go for the quick fix of adding nails or soaking it in antifreeze.

Antifreeze and Hammer Heads

While I'm on the topic of antifreeze, a lot of jewelers dip the handle into anti-freeze to permanently swell and tighten hammer heads. Twenty years ago, I thought this was a cool little tip. Today, I know too much to appreciate this chemical. Be aware that anti-freeze is extremely poisonous to animal life and toxic to our sewer and septic system. If you live near the ocean, like I do, it can easily make its way into the water and stress our delicate oceanic ecosystem even further. Antifreeze (and certain brands of windshield wiper fluid) is so toxic to dogs and certain breeds with low body fat (like my borzoi) that if they even step into it, they can die from poisoning. Ethylene glycol tastes sweet, which is why so many animals (dogs, cats, birds, and rabbits) are attracted to it, whether in the parking lot or a jeweler's studio.

That's why I try to rid my daily life of dangerous chemicals, not just because of what I might do, but also because of what someone else might accidentally get into. For the outcome of the story, use the following meta tags to Google: antifreeze, Arkansas, day care, windshield wiper fluid, Beasley Allen.

An aside: When I was in eighth grade, my best friend Cheri used to draw beautiful horses. All I managed to doodle over and over were mazes and skulls with crossbones. Who knew that someday, as a professional, it would pay off!

Kiln Brick: Soft

You'll have to visit a *real* ceramic supply place to purchase a soft kiln brick. By real, I mean the type of store that sells bricks to build your own kiln. These are specific bricks that aid in fusing because, as a refractory material, they reflect heat back onto your work. I've tried various soldering bricks and pads and, other than the jeweler's charcoal block, still prefer this type of brick. They are fragile (you can stick your fingernail into them) and shed brick dust. Avoid breathing it as you would avoid breathing any dust or dirt. I use a K-26 brick, which is rated to 2600°F. It is a straight brick and measures: 2 1/2 X 4 1/2 X 9 inches. Don't settle for anything smaller.

Care and Feeding

If you don't drop it, it will last decades. I keep mine wrapped up in thin bubble wrap and store it in a chocolate tin. What a great excuse to buy and eat more chocolate!

Do not use the broad brick surface for anything other than fusing. Substances such as flux (for soldering) will contaminate it. Flux turns to glass when heated, then melts onto your piece and into the porous brick. When you remove your piece the brick comes with it creating holes and an uneven surface which is bad for fusing.

Re-planing

Besides the great refractory quality and larger work area, another advantage to the soft kiln brick is that you can easily re-plane it. Over time it will chip and develop holes. Because of its thick, compact shape, you can re-plane it several times without losing any of its structural integrity.

In August of 2007, I was visiting my mother in North Carolina. My brick had gotten banged up in the suitcase because TSA (airport security) didn't replace the lid of the tin it was stored in. It wasn't in good enough shape for flat fusing due to the uneven surface. I remember sitting in Mom's living room, gazing outside, wondering if there was a simple way to smooth it back down. My eyes wandered through the backyard, and bingo! The cement parking pad was perfect. Holding the brick with both hands, I scraped it back and forth on the cement like you

might hold a scrub brush to clean the kitchen floor. In less than a minute, the cement sanded the brick as smooth as new! Water from a hose safely drove the brick dust into the grass to become one with the soil.

Mallets

A mallet looks like a hammer but it is made out of softer materials such as rubber, plastic, or rolled-up leather.

When I was a jewelry professor in South Georgia, I traveled a lot. Once, when laying out my tools to pack, I noticed my dog Eve's ears go up in such a way that I knew she was up to something. I fol-

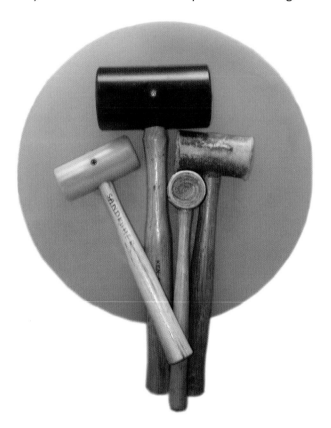

lowed her gaze to the tool box, curious what she was excited about. Turned out, she had her eye on the leather mallet. To her, the rolled-up leather was just an expensive chew toy on a stick. That explained the curious impressions I'd noticed on it!

The goal of a mallet is to shape and harden your project without leaving behind the marks that a steel hammer would. You can use it to stretch metal, such as a ring on a tapered ring mandrel, without marking it up. If you use the mallet to hammer your piece on steel, it will stretch faster than if you use a wooden or plastic block. Many jewelers have a cleaned and de-barked tree stump in their studio that serves as a good base. Tree stumps can also be custom-carved with negative shapes to form your project. Just make sure you get a fresh stump to avoid bringing insects (such as termites) into your studio.

Mouse Pad
(Phone Book and Grippy Fabric)

That's right: a mouse pad. Use this item to help dampen both the sound and vibratory impact to the hand, arm, and shoulder when hammering on a steel block. Depending on the composition of the mouse pad, it may also help grip the steel block and prevent it from walking across your work surface as you cathartically whale away on your project with the hammer.

If you don't have access to a mouse pad, a telephone book (remember those?) is also a great option. It also raises your work by providing a stage.

Don't forget, making jewelry is messy work. Steel blocks are tougher than stainless steel blocks, but they need oiling to prevent rusting. The oil will transfer to the mouse pad, so don't use it for your computer mouse afterward. It will also transfer to your metal, but you can easily remove it with blue Dawn® dishwashing soap and a dedicated, used toothbrush. Baby toothbrushes are extra soft.

Another related item is the rubbery, synthetic fabric that is sold in a roll to cut and put under throw rugs and keep them from sliding. This soft, mesh, grippy fabric is sold in hardware, drug, and department stores. Use it under your steel block to keep it in place. You won't need much. I place the leftovers on the jeep's console to stabilize my dog's paws when she rides shotgun.

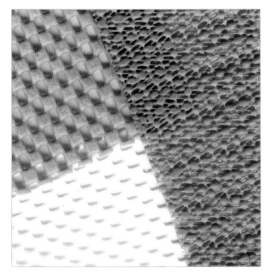

Common, synthetic grip fabric is a great product to use with your mouse pad or phone book to keep the steel block from walking across your work bench when hammering.

Pliers
Three That I Can't Live Without

Flush Cutter

OK, maybe technically this isn't really a pair of pliers, but rather, a cutter. Since it handles like a pair of pliers, I consider it one of the trilogy that I religiously carry with me.

Compare the flat (flush) side of these flush cutters to the valley side. When you orient your cutters, remember the valley side cuts the sharp wire ends.

How is this tool different from ordinary wire cutters? Regular wire cutters leave a sharp tip on the wire. Flush cutters leave a blunt (flush) edge. If you hold a set of flush cutters closed and examine both sides, you will see that one side is a flat plane, while the other side has a valley. The flat side cuts flush. The valley side cuts the sharp tip when it is against the wire. By contrast, when you close a regular pair of wire cutters, both sides have a valley and no matter which way you turn the cutter, it will leave a sharp end on your wire.

Flush cutters should be reserved for times when you need to flush cut. For general wire cutting, I recommend using regular wire cutters from the hardware store or the cutting well in the rosary pliers. Flush cutters are meant for use on dead-soft metals, such as sterling, silver, copper, brass, gold, gold fill. Never, ever use them on (bead) stringing wire or household projects. Flush cutters are often expensive, precision tools that can dull fast, so it's wise to keep them out of reach from well meaning kids, spouses, or classmates!

When I consider buying a new set of flush cutters, or checking if old ones need replacement, I close them, run my fingernail across the flat plane and see if there is a big "step" (place where my fingernail gets caught). The larger the step, the more "out of true" (torqued) they are. All flush cutters have a little bit of a step. Just avoid the ones with the big steps.

Whenever possible, I use the entire blade (not just the tip) to wear the cutter more evenly and extend the life of the tool. Depending on the manufacturer, they may offer to re-sharpen them for a fee.

I have one pair of flush cutters saved for show-and-tell. This pair was used to cut stringing wire. Note the hole in the blade. The tips were used to cut something equally as tough. Note how the tips are splayed away from each other. Stainless steel also makes weaker blades.

Needle-nose Chain Pliers

Why they call these "chain" pliers, I don't know. If I were trapped on a desert island with one set of pliers to make chains with, it would be the rosary pliers, not these. It is nearly impossible to make chains with these pliers because you can't form a round loop with them, since the legs are not round in shape. They are good, however, at holding onto metal and opening/closing jump rings that make up a chain. Perhaps that's where they get their name.

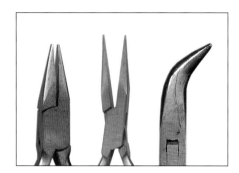

Three styles of needle-nose chain pliers: short, long, and curved.

There are many different tip styles. I always carry at least two with me which helps, for example, when closing jump rings: one to passively hold the link while the other does the wiggling/closing. Ultimately, I recommend purchasing all three of these styles:

- Short chain-nose pliers with a jaw length approximately 1 inch. These are strong, stocky, and less likely to torque, and will last a long time. Use them to hold on tight to your project.
- Long chain-nose pliers with jaw length approximately 1 1/2 inches will get you into hard-to-reach places. The longer the jaw length, the more difficult to hold onto your piece.
- The curved chain-nose pliers are commonly used in beading. The curve in the pliers hugs the curve of a bead when you are finishing a closed coil (hanged man's noose, wire wrap or briolette wrap). I find them handy for many other situations as well.

New needle-nose chain pliers often have a sharp edge to them that can easily mark up softer metals such as fine silver. Use your mill smooth file to gently take down the harsh edge to a more rounded feel. How do you know if you've done it right? Run your finger across the edge of your needle-nose chain pliers before and after you file. It's more reliable than looking at it for confirmation.

Rosary Pliers

I prefer rosary pliers to round-nose pliers because they have everything a round-nose plier has, plus a cutting well. This feature allows you to work faster when making rosary loops, because you don't need to put them down and pick up an additional pair of wire cutters. Basically, it's two tools in one. I also like the heft of the German version.

Some people fall in love with their cars. I fall in love with my tools. I've used this German style of rosary pliers since the mid-1980s and have never been disappointed. The red handle used to symbolize quality to me. Recently I noticed other brands have adopted the red-handled "look."

You'll need these pliers to form round loops, to curl up wire, and for general wire cutting. When you buy them, make sure the tapered (cone-shaped) legs do not have teeth on them for gripping metal. The hardware store version (as opposed to a jewelry store version) often has teeth that will mar your work.

Are the tapered legs bow-legged? Close the pliers. Examine the base of the cone-shaped legs. Is there a noticeable gap between the legs? If yes, this will create a problem when you are trying to grab wire using the base of the legs; the wire will fall through. There was a lapidary shop in San Francisco that gave me a really good deal on a dozen rosary pliers. Delighted at how cheap they were, my joy quickly soured when, faced with a class full of students, I discovered the basic flaw: the wire would fall through the bowlegged gap when we attempted to make rosary loops. Call me naive but, why would you manufacture rosary pliers that can't make rosary loops?

Are the cone-shaped legs round, or do they have a flat spot inside where they meet? If they have a flat spot on the inside, they will create a flat spot on any rounded loops that you attempt to make.

Legend has it that these are called rosary pliers because nuns use them to make rosary loops with. One of my students at the San Mateo Community College Community Education workshops joked that if you're an atheist, you can call them *rosemary* pliers. I live in such a great multi-culti place!

Rags

You might be wondering why I'm writing about something as mundane as a rag, but you'd be surprised at what I've seen folks use. A rag should be very clean, absorbent, and not fall apart.

Why clean? Because many contaminants can interfere with your work processes. While 3-in-1 household oil (or mayonnaise from your lunch) is an obvious residue that may interfere with many processes such as fusing, something as seemingly innocuous as hand lotion can be just as detrimental. Sand, bits of metal, and other debris can scratch your work. Bacteria can get transferred into crevices of your project and start developing like a little petri dish on your piece of jewelry. Nice conceptual art!

I also find that if I use a cloth for just one project or specific task, I can usually put it in with my regular laundry to wash. Of course, heavily loaded and soiled rags need to be separated from regular laundry so as not to contaminate it!

I always keep two stacks of clean rags on hand. They are recycled from old T-shirts, sweatpants, dishcloths, and kitchen towels.

If I know I have a particularly messy project coming up, it's really convenient to wear a pair of old blue jeans. Analogous to painter's pants, I use them to wipe my hands on! Using the top of the thigh, for example, provides a great place to lay a project while hand polishing. They also provide a psychological transition into metalsmithing work mode.

Viva la clean rags!

Even though the rags in this photo are very clean, such things as dried acrylic paint (from painting) or T-shirt logos can scratch metal. So if a mirror finish is what you are looking for, only use soft rags.

Ruler

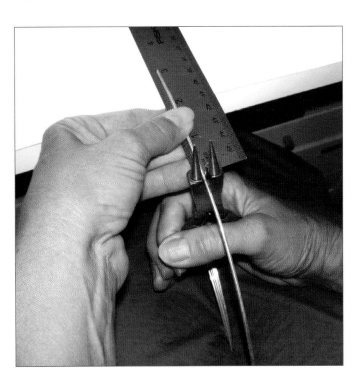

My favorite ruler is metal and doesn't have a margin. I use metal in case I'm measuring something that's still a little too hot and may melt plastic or burn wood. Yes, I get impatient, but do as I say, not as I do. Margins are an issue because you can't begin to measure at the end of the ruler, like you can with a tape measure. If you use a ruler without a margin, it's one less thing to have to pay attention to and commit to memory.

If I have to cut a lot of wire, I want to work as efficiently as possible. Here is how to do it:

1. Hang the beginning of the ruler over the edge of the table or work bench, toward you.
2. Sit directly in front of it.
3. Clamp the coil of wire vertically between your knees.
4. Feed the wire's end up onto the ruler and measurement mark.
5. Press the wire flat, with your thumb against the ruler.
6. Orient the rosary pliers with the handles down toward the floor and the cutting well facing you.
7. Press the flat part of the rosary pliers against the (overhanging) end of the ruler.
8. Cut your length of wire.

Screw Punch

During the 1980s, I went to an Andreas Vollenweider concert. His harp was the central instrument, but sounded largely like electronically made New Age music. As he came out on stage, he asked us, "What happens when the electricity goes out?" This political comment introduced the "unplugged" version of his music.

I have often asked myself the same question when pondering the accessibility of many types of tools and equipment. What happens when the electricity goes out? With the right tools, nothing; you can just keep on working! I was fortunate enough to learn metalsmithing in a high-tech studio. We had lots of expensive tools and equipment at our disposal. The problem was that I'd never studied how people used to make intricate jewelry before they had things like burn-out ovens, vacuum casters, drill presses, sonic cleaners, tumblers, polishing machines, rolling mills, and oxy-acetylene tanks. Once I graduated from college, I was overwhelmed with the financial reality of what I would have to buy to emulate the studio that I'd spent five-plus years in.

One highlight in my simplification journey (now a teaching philosophy) was when I was driving home to Georgia after studying fusing in New York City in September of 1996. I was planning to visit my mother in Wilmington, North Carolina, and the road trip became a race to reach her home before hurricane Fran hit the East Coast. When nearing Raleigh, my mother called and advised me to wait until the storm passed because they were evacuating. My friend Lillian invited me to stay over. Turned out that a few hours after crashing into Wilmington, Fran hit us in Raleigh.

The chaotic aftermath made it impossible for me to leave Lillian and Randy's home in Raleigh for a week. I'd always wished to be marooned on a desert island with all of my jewelry tools and projects. Problem was, I forgot to include electricity in my fantasy. The land was so saturated with water that the trees fell in the hurricane's gale, taking their roots with them and leaving open pits everywhere. One tree took out their front porch. Power lines were lying everywhere, some precariously close to my street-parked car. No electricity meant no lights or air conditioning (temperatures hovering in the nineties with 100 percent humidity), and no power tools to finish my very first beach glass bracelet.

All I needed was to drill some holes in the backs of a few more pieces of sheet metal. So much for

all this high-tech knowledge, foiled for one small detail: electricity. Lillian had the solution: an industrial punch. It's similar to a paper puncher, but it's heavy duty and works great on metal. Voilà! No electricity needed.

This was the seed that got me thinking about simpler, alternative ways of working with metal. These days, I travel-teach all over the place, and classrooms are usually not even close to being a jeweler's studio. I've adopted a low-tech lifestyle so that I can schlep everything that I need with me in trains, planes, and automobiles. Instead of a drill press, flexible shaft, dremel tool, or regular power drill, I have three types of metal hole punchers that fill all my needs: the screw punch (my favorite), industrial punch, and hole punch pliers. None of them use electricity, plus I also don't have to worry about the renegade bit drilling into a student's hand.

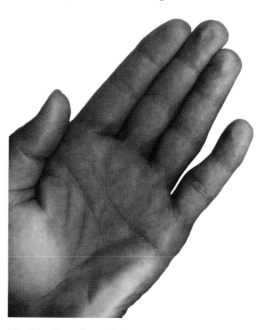

My friends call me OSHA Iris because I'm so safety conscious. What they don't realize is that I speak from experience. Look closely at the palm of my hand. See that little grey spot? That happened late one evening when I was tired but wanted to drill just one more thing. The drill bit from my flexible shaft slipped and I drilled right into my hand, taking the sterling shavings and 3-in-1 household oil with it. Now this "tattoo" is a gentle reminder of what power tools can do. It also helped fuel my enthusiasm for my hole punch tools that do not require electricity or an off switch.

In my personal creative life, I like keeping things simple and portable. The more you own, the more you have to worry about. When you buy your screw punch, make sure you read the specifications on what types and thickness of metal you can use it on. To store it, make sure the screws are screwed all the way down (closed) so it won't get damaged knocking up against the other tools in your tool box.

Steel Block

Care and Feeding

Steel blocks rust so it is important that you save the cardboard box and oil paper that your steel block is shipped in. Add 3-In-One® household oil to the paper and keep it wrapped around the block when not in use.

What happens if you ignore the rust that is slowly taking over your steel block? It will get hammered right into your project, causing a permanent blemish. To remove rust, you can send it out to a local machine shop to have it re-planed, or touch it up yourself if the damage isn't too invasive. Use steel wool from the hardware store (not Brillo® pads from the grocery store as they contain soap) to scrub the spot with oil. Rub off with a clean rag.

Safety Issues

I've marked "top" and "bottom" on my steel block box with a permanent marker, so I don't accidentally pick it up upside down and have the heavy block with sharp corners land on my feet. I also keep a fat rubber band wrapped tightly around it for transportation. The oil from the box will deteriorate the rubber band faster than normal, so keep an eye on it.

To preserve your ears, consider wearing earplugs when you hammer. If you're ears are "ringing" (tinnitus) after you're finished, it means that they probably have experienced some damage.

Scrap Jars

The byproduct of working with metal is scraps. I save mine in small jars such as the type that baby food or artichoke hearts come in. Save that receipt for a tax write-off. Wrap the cleaned jar and lid with tape, then use a permanent marker to label what type of metal you are collecting.

If you have a scrap jar full of fine silver and you get just one piece of sterling in there, it becomes contaminated. If you try to fuse the fine silver scraps, the copper in the sterling will interfere. If you accidentally get some fine silver into the sterling jar, it won't contaminate sterling, but will give it a higher silver content. This won't help you much in terms of less tarnishing or more value.

Besides fine- and sterling silver, I also have jars of copper, brass, and different kinds of gold. I use scraps in many of my workshops so I've never had the need to send them in to a refinery. Playing with scraps is a great way to fire up the imagination.

Jewelry metal refineries prefer separated scraps (more value) and will either give you credit toward stock (sheet, wire, tubing, etc.) or cash back. The market value of the metal combined with their service fee determines how much money you'll get in exchange, so it's beneficial to wait until the market is in your favor. It's also good to shop around for the best rates. To prevent theft and damage (creating loss of materials), many companies have a protocol in terms of packaging and shipping, so do your research before sending anything out.

In class, we collect the scraps in the clean corners of our cookie sheets so brick dust isn't mixed in. When traveling, I put scraps in small jewelry bags. At the studio, they go into clear glass jars, which are better for viewing. I always want to use that scrap the size of an angel-on-a-head pin located at the bottom of the jar.

Tripod and Screen

This is an awesome tool to elevate and heat your projects from underneath. The tripod is easy to transport because it breaks down into parts. The legs unscrew from the ring platform. The tripod usually comes with two types of screen: thick and thin. Both screens are relatively minor heat sinks so they won't pull the heat away from your jewelry projects while you are trying to heat them up. I use the tripod to elevate work for accessibility and fire safety.

Preparing Your Screen

I've gone through a lot of tools during my teaching career. When I first bought tripods, they were good to go. Then one year, I bought a bunch of new ones and brought them into class. Remember, things change! The new, thinner screens were all shiny and pretty. Enter teacher's nightmare here: As my students began using their torch and tripods to heat their delicately and meticulously set-up bezels, the shiny screens started giving off a toxic-looking yellow smoke. Not only did it freak all of us out, it coated and contaminated their projects with a yellow substance that interfered with soldering. It was a disaster.

Now I take my students outside and show them how to hold the screens in their cross-lock tweezers safely and burn off a small section on which to work on top. We always do this over cement and avoid breathing the smoke. I don't know what that shiny coating on the screens is, and I only burn off just enough to use, because it doesn't look healthy for our atmosphere. Wish they'd bring the old, unglamorous mesh back.

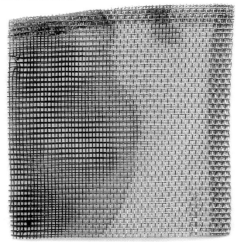

Tumbler: Homemade

In January 2007, I traveled to Wilmington, North Carolina to visit with my mother while she was going in for knee surgery. What was supposed to be a one-week visit turned into a month because she contracted hospital-acquired pneumonia. I suddenly had a lot of time on my hands and metalsmithing was a productive distraction. My good friend Lillian came down from Raleigh for emotional support and what we call professional development.

Even though we don't look alike, Lillian is like my twin because our interests, mannerisms, timing, tastes in food, etc., are so similar, it's uncanny. Lillian was also a fine arts major in college, and we both segued into the field of professional jewelry after graduating. Not long after me, she too discovered the convenience of the butane torch.

Lillian brought a bunch of tools and supplies down to Wilmington to teach me the Diagonal Thai weave. Afterwards we were brainstorming on how we could create a homemade tumbler. We pictured something low tech and cheap. What if we just put the 2.5 lbs. of stainless steel, mixed-shaped shot into a plastic jar and shook it? I dug through my mother's cabinets looking for a soft plastic container, since hard plastic would be more likely to get brittle and break. I found a (recycling #7) Dole pineapple container that was perfect for the amount of shot and project size. We put the shot in, added just enough water to cover everything, and added a teaspoon of blue Dawn® detergent. The Thai weave bracelet is pure silver (no beads), so we traded off, shaking it like crazy on the way to the beach. Besides the harsh sound (you might consider earplugs), it was fun and when we arrived at the beach fifteen minutes later and examined the bracelet, it was sparkling and work-hardened. Our grassroots effort worked.

Since then, I've bravely experimented with more fragile jewelry. I've learned that I can gently place a beaded necklace in the homemade tumbler and instead of shaking it like a martini; I can rock it back and forth horizontally like a baby. So far, this method has polished lots of projects, including beads and gemstones, without breaking them. Whether or not it works for you depends on the quality of beads that you are using, patience when shuffling it, and above all, experimentation.

Tweezers

Long Cross-Lock Tweezers

I prefer long, straight, cross-lock tweezers because they have no parts that can fall off, and you can use them in any orientation (lay them on any side). These tweezers lock onto the piece that you are handling and heating. If they get repeatedly annealed (heated to a dull orange glow), they will soften and the tips will gradually move apart. At that point, they will no longer tweeze. No worries! They are meant to be abused. Use your needle-nose chain pliers to bend the tips back so they touch.

For production work (such as the Matchstick Tier project), it's handy to have two cross-lock tweezers. While one is cooling, you can use the other. By alternating tweezers, you work faster.

Don't ever consider using pliers to hold pieces that are being heated. It is unsafe for you and the pliers. Pliers are shorter, which puts your hand closer to the torch flame. What's worse than burning your hand? Melting the plastic on the plier handle into your skin! Heating the pliers' tips will also anneal and ruin them. You can tell if they have been heated if they are blue or grey. Pliers are also a greater heat sink and will interfere with heating your piece. For the cost of replacing pliers, you can buy several tweezers.

AA Tweezers

These precision tweezers are made to be strong and pick up very small bits. I use them to move grains around (granulation) and to place little pieces of copper when alloy fusing. Do not heat them, because their delicate tips will anneal very quickly and then be ruined.

Warning
When working with the tools and materials referenced in this book, it is imperative that you read the manufacturer's directions, heed warnings and seek prompt medical attention in the case of injury. Since technology evolves over time, don't be shy about rereading these with every new purchase.

Butane Gas

As a college student in 1982, I learned how to make jewelry using oxy-acetylene torches. In the 1990s when I moved to the San Francisco Bay Area and into a cramped urban space, I had to rethink what it meant to live with, use, transport and fill my acetylene tank.

These gas tanks are illegal to carry around in a car due to potential "pooling" of leaky gas in an enclosed space. If you get into an accident: KABOOM! To transport them legally, your state probably requires you to strap them into an open truck bed. You can check with your local tank-filling (welding) business. My problem was that I owned a Nissan and didn't have any open-truck-bed friends so my acetylene tank was no longer convenient.

It's also a little nerve wracking to live with tanks of gas. What if there is a fire or if, like me, you live in earthquake country? If the regulator breaks off, the tank becomes a rocket. Don Duncan, my professor at Ohio State University, described an acetylene tank on the loose as being like an escaping balloon, except the tanks can go through six feet of concrete. Never underestimate the power of stupidity. Check out what can happen when someone else causes the fire, but you are the one with an acetylene tank in your studio: http://www.sandkuhler.com/workshops_safety.html.

Another issue is insurance. Chances are your renter's/homeowners insurance doesn't cover the gas tank(s). Even if you aren't responsible for starting the fire that set your building alight, your insurance may not cover the results. On the other hand, it probably covers your crème brûlée torch!

When I moved to the Bay Area, I strapped my acetylene tank up in the garage, which was fairly safe but still part of the house. Have you tried working in a garage? It is the most uninspiring place: cavernous, cold, dirty, and full of spiders.

Switching to a butane torch liberated me from the garage. I was freer to work on tables in the rest of the house, as well as taking the show on the road and teaching in ordinary classrooms and retail venues. After a year of not using my acetylene tank, I sold it.

Since butane is also lighter fluid, you can find it in lots of different retail spaces, particularly places that sell cigarettes and lighters. In California, I can find butane at kitchen supply-, drug-, hardware-, and service station stores. I always recommend getting the biggest can so you have more (ahem) bang for your buck.

Chewing Gum

No kidding. When I go to class, I bring a bag of various flavors and brands of gum for my students. Could it be because when I was a child, I was always getting in trouble for chewing gum in class? Perhaps. But recently they've come out with studies that suggest for some personality types, it helps foster focus. I know that when I find myself in a classroom trying to absorb new knowledge, the two things that help me focus are doodling and chewing gum. Gum also came in handy once when a torch foot kept falling off in the middle of fusing. (Save that torch receipt).

Blue Dawn® Dishwashing Soap

To clean your metal, you need a good strong detergent that doesn't have a bunch of chemicals in it that can react to or contaminate metal. It also has to be blue. Why blue? Because, believe it or not, the color of soap will color your metal. It's particularly obvious with white metals such as silver. Blue makes white look whiter. That's why you'll find it in our laundry detergent (whether powder or liquid), in our toothpaste, and, in some cultures, eye drops! Dawn® was also the soap they used to clean the oil off wildlife during the oil spills. For a while, Dawn® referenced this through a drawing of waterfowl on its bottle. Stay away from yellow, pink, or green, which will make your hard work look dingy.

Earplugs

Huh? What d'you say? I'm sorry, I can't hear you 'cause I've lost my hearing range due to hammering without wearing earplugs. I'm also cranky from not getting much sleep 'cause my ears ring all night. You can find earplugs at your local hardware or drug store, plus any communal hiking hut with a gift shop. Just look for them next to the poison oak salve.

Oil

I took a workshop once at a jewelry studio and witnessed someone using lip balm as a drilling lubricant. Repeatedly using the wrong oil or lubricant can cause metals to weaken and unexpectedly break down, which could have disastrous results. Stick with 3-In-One® brand household oil for tools and you can't go wrong. It works well on squeaky doors, too.

Patination

Keep in mind that a patina occurs naturally over time and in certain climatic and chemical conditions. Different metals and alloys react differently in terms of color, the amount of time to develop, and the conditions to maintain those colors. Ultimately, patinas are unstable and will change over time.

The easiest patina to create and maintain is black (antiquing) on copper and silver. All of the methods below will turn your jewelry dark-brown to black and, once you add highlights with a polishing cloth, you will have added visual depth. Occasionally, you may get a peacock-colored reaction, but it won't be permanent. Be careful about exposing beads or gemstones to patination chemicals because they can damage or stain (or stink) them. Experiment first.

Boiled Egg Method

Buy the smallest plastic container that can fit your project plus two halves of an egg lying open. Make sure the container is transparent and has a tight-fitting plastic lid. Find eggs that have a really yellow yolk, which is your clue that they have high sulfur content. Next buy a large pizza and have it delivered (another great tax write-off). Eat the pizza but save the little white plastic table thingy in the middle.

While the egg is boiling, put the pizza table thingy on its back in the plastic container. Place your jewelry on top of its legs. There should be minimal contact. At ten minutes your egg is hard boiled. Pour off the water and with a rag, hold the egg so you don't burn yourself. Crack it wide open and immediately put it into the plastic container. Close the lid and no peeking for twenty-four hours. The heat and sulfur fumes will work their magic.

Liver of Sulfur

If exposed to moisture and sunlight, liver of sulfur spoils. That's why, when you buy it in rock form, it comes in a metal can. To use it, heat some water in a dedicated ceramic cup, just under boiling. Add a pea-sized piece of liver of sulfur. Dip the piece to be patinated in for about ten seconds. You should see it turn black. Rinse and dry.

You might be able to save the liquid liver of sulfur if you store it in an airtight non-metal container. Wrap it in black plastic and place it in the back of a dark cabinet. Remember, sunlight spoils it. Make sure the can that the rocks came in is tightly shut. I also put it in a ziplock bag just to prevent further air/moisture exchange.

Hot Springs

My favorite way of turning silver and copper black is to spend some R & R at a hot springs. Just follow your nose to find the correct conditions. Sulfur springs are also great for psoriasis, but they will leave your hair smelling stinky for days; just like seriously medicated dandruff shampoos, which can also patina your jewelry. Look for a shampoo that lists (root word) sulfur as one of the first ingredients. Plan to tweak your experiment a lot with heat and rehydration over a period of days for best results. Great tax write-offs.

Cheater Patina

There is a store where I teach that doesn't have windows that open. The owner is sensitive to smells, so we've never used patina. One day, while we were working on a project in the small classroom, I decided to enhance my class samples using a permanent marker. Wearing latex gloves, I coated the entire project in black, then highlighted it with a polishing pad. The results looked like an authentic patina. One could argue that underneath that permanent marker, the piece is on its way to becoming authentically patinated anyway, so it's not really cheating.

Permanent Marker

This is one of those materials that I always have with me. You'll never know when you need to mark your piece of jewelry for some measurement, and water-based markers won't stick. Fine-point Sharpies® are my favorite. Several years ago another brand surfaced that advertised as being non-toxic

Whether a sulfur rock, liver of sulfur, medicated shampoo, sulfur hot springs, or a boiled egg; if it smells stinky good like a rotten egg, it has the power to patinate your silver and copper.

and permanent, but now I can't find them any more. Things change! There may be another all natural brand that pops up again so keep an eye out. For Sharpies®, alcohol works best to remove the permanent marker from metal. Of course, don't forget to put the cap back on right away to prevent it from drying out in-between uses.

Polishing Pads

I like using the little white, 2 X 2 inch polishing pads that don't seem to have a consistent name from distributor to distributor. I've seen them called Pro-polish Pads or just polishing pads. Of course, now that I've described them, they'll change the shape and color. They are spongy in texture and have a very light abrasion. The results are immediate and, with enough elbow grease, they bring out a mirror finish. Note that they do not remove scratches, but the finish is so shiny that the reflection can distract the eye from picking up minor scratches. Once the pad is completely covered in metal, it will stop working.

Some polishing cloths fall apart or give off a linty dust (impregnated with polishing compounds), which I suspect is not healthy to breathe or to have settle in your environment. Mostly, I don't like getting in front of polishing wheels to use the traditional compounds such as tripoli and rouge, so I'll use just about any other method to texture and polish my pieces.

3M® also has a nice group of micro sandpapers that give a frosty finish. Because things change, experiment and see what the market is coming up with next.

Wire Concepts
Temper, Temper, Temper

Resist the urge to play with (or straighten) your wire. If you own a wire straightening tool, hide it from this book.

Here's why: When metals are mined from the earth, they are often melted to separate and clean out all impurities. The act of heating metal softens and anneals it. The result is a temper that we refer to as dead soft. That means the metal is as soft (malleable or ductile) as possible.

When the dead-soft metal is formed into stock, it is hardened and stressed. Rolling it out into a sheet or pulling it into a wire causes the microstructure to become work hardened. The metal will become springy and, with continued work hardening, it will become so brittle that it breaks.

When you were a child, did you ever try breaking a metal coat hanger? After you picked a spot and began bending it back and forth, three things happened: 1) The bend becomes hot (due to stress). 2) The spot wants to move over to where it's softer. 3) The wire breaks.

My college professor Don Duncan at Ohio State University also described the process like this: Back in the old days, television repairmen would make house calls. Their van was filled with things that could fix televisions such as test tubes and wire. One of the problems they encountered was that the wire lived in the back of the van and would be driven around day after day. The act of driving vibrated (bounced) everything. This is equivalent to a thousand little elves hammering away on the wire. Just sitting there on the spools, the wires would become work hardened. What happened when the repairman tried to use the wire? It would crack and break.

I use dead soft wire for all my projects because within the dead soft wire lies the potential for half hard and hard. In other words, if I need half hard or hard wire, I only have to twist, bend, or use a mallet or wire straightener on my dead soft wire. On the other hand, to make hard or half hard wire dead soft, I have to anneal it – bring it up to a dull-orange glow, which is a lot more work. I would just rather buy dead soft. I also think that dead soft is kinder to your hands (think carpal tunnel) and tools.

PROJECTS

The topics in this book were selected and written to build on each other in terms of complexity. Several projects and/or techniques can be mixed and matched. For example, use the Matchstick Tier lesson to draw a bead (ball up wire), then combine with the Briolette Wrap to form head pins. Test the size of the bead/gemstone's hole to determine the gauge of the wire. I measure my head pins at 2 inches after I've drawn the bead. For a more decorative effect, use three head pins at once, as shown.

Lucky Horseshoe Charm Bracelet

One of my students lives near Quincy, California. She loves to ride horses and suggested I hold a jewelry retreat at nearby Greenhorn Creek Guest Ranch. To prepare for the first class in November of 2008, I dropped by the ranch and took lots of inspiring photos to research and develop a customized project.

The manager, Lisa Kelly, gave me a great tour of the grounds. There was a pile of horseshoes by the stables. Intrigued, I asked if I could have a couple. What attracted me was the infinite variety I saw within the basic horseshoe design. They came in all sizes, some shiny and brand new, while others were rusted, in various stages of deterioration. Others were misshapen and beaten-up looking. Those horseshoes were infused with history.

I left with a pair of used horseshoes that became the jumping-off point for designing a similarly shaped link. After some trial and error, I was able to figure out a system to connect the horseshoe links into a chain.

Since horseshoe images are often used as a symbol for good luck, I decided to expand on that theme for the scope of my workshop. By using simple tools and wire techniques to capture charms and found objects, students could express their individuality. In addition, the act of choosing charms is also a great venue for discussion about personal iconography, content, and the creative process.

Two used horseshoes from the Greenhorn Guest Ranch in Quincy, California, serve as inspiration for a chain design and workshop.

Tools Checklist
- Flush cutter
- Forming/planishing hammer
- Mouse pad
- Needle-nose chain pliers
- Gauge
- Glasses
- Rosary pliers
- Ruler
- Screw punch (to punch holes in thin, soft metal found objects)
- Steel block
- 3/4 inch dowel rod

Materials Checklist
- Beads, trinkets, charms, found objects, totems
- Chewing gum
- Earplugs
- Polishing pads
- 1 inch, 20- or 22-gauge wire for briolette wrap per object
- 3 feet, 12-gauge wire (14-gauge if you have weak hands)

These three horseshoe bracelets are made from fine silver and copper. Charms include (from the left) fluorite crystal bead, found mother-of-pearl, copper sheet ace, found ring, patinated found object, copper sheet bird, silver-colored metal beach garbage, sea-shell with interesting hole, and mother of pearl-star-bead.

Getting Started

Use your rosary pliers to cut nine wire sticks of 12-gauge wire into 3-inch pieces. Nine is the approximate amount of links that you will need to make an average-sized bracelet.

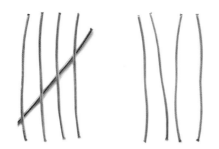

Cut 12-gauge wire into nine 3-inch pieces.

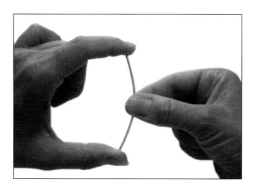

Use two hands to pull/squeeze the wire pieces into a teardrop shape.

Teardrops

A quick and easy way to bend your wire (once you get the hang of it) is to use your index finger and thumb to hold a wire by the ends. With the other hand, use your thumb and index finger to pinch the center of the wire and pull. As you pull the wire with one hand, push the ends together with the other. Pay attention to whether the shape is collapsing symmetrically. If not, adjust the pressure and location of where you are pinching the wire.

Following are instructions on how to hammer and connect the chain. One way is to complete each horseshoe link, then assemble them by opening the curls. The other way is to make and link them as you go. I find both approaches helpful. To focus on your shaping, I recommend that you complete two links and fit them together before making more. That way, if you need to adjust your technique, you still have seven more chances for improvement!

All nine wires are bent in half until the tips are touching.

Hammering

Coming from a fine arts background (and appreciating feng shui), I often ponder the symbolic implications of what image I'm hammering on. The target graphics on my mouse pads probably, subconsciously, help me aim. Many of my students consider hammering a cathartic experience. What sort of image gets you excited enough that you don't notice your exercise-induced fatigue? Did you know that you can order customized mouse pads with photos? How about one with your favorite "love to hate" theme such as the great floating vortex of plastic garbage in the Open Ocean, or a photo of your ex? Just a thought.

You'll have to hold your link in order to control it while you hammer. I'm right handed, so I hold it with my left hand and use my right to hammer. Use the planishing side of the hammer to flatten slightly more than half of the horseshoe shape. Leave the tips untouched so they aren't work hardened. These will be formed (curled) to hook into the next link.

If the horseshoe shape begins to open up as you hammer it, use your fingers to squeeze it closed again. Avoid hammering excessively on the edge of the wire, because it will become razor sharp.

After you've hammered the wire into the desired width, use the forming (rounded) side of the hammer to add dappled marks. Once polished, these marks will catch and reflect light like shimmering sunlight on water!

A teardrop, ready to hammer.

The ends of the horseshoe are not hammered.

Forming Horseshoe Links

Use your rosary pliers to curl-and butt-up both ends of the wire. How far down the cone-shaped plier legs you work determines how big (or small) the curl will be. Rosary pliers come in different sizes, so you have to experiment to see what works for you.

The curl has to be large enough to comfortably accommodate the hammered part of the next link. Don't be surprised if you have to readjust the first few links until you get the bugs worked out. Soon, you'll move through the process like a well-oiled production line.

Line the curl up directly below the horseshoe shape so you don't see it from the top (bird's-eye view). Double-check that the curl is really closed; this will help place and dictate the finished shape of the curled links later when you hook them up into a chain.

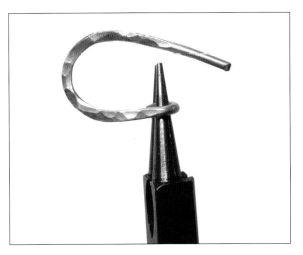

1. Use rosary pliers to curl-and butt-up both ends of the wire.

2. How far down the cone-shaped plier legs you work determines how big (or small) the curl will be.

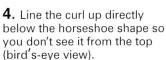

3. The curl has to be large enough to comfortably accommodate the hammered part of the next link. Rosary pliers come in different sizes: experiment to see what works for you.

4. Line the curl up directly below the horseshoe shape so you don't see it from the top (bird's-eye view).

Concept: Opening the Door of a Plane

In class, I use a discussion about doors as an analogy to help students understand working in multiple planes. When a door is closed, it is in the same plane as the wall that contains it. When you open the door, it opens into a different plane. Whether you are imagining a door that you walk through or a trap door in the floor or ceiling, they all open into a different plane compared to when they are closed. (A door that opens *in* the same plane as the wall that contains it is a track, pocket, or sliding door. I'm not referring to those.)

Use the needle-nose chain pliers to open the curled loop of the horseshoe link sideways and out of plane. This prepares it for getting hooked into the next link while preserving the nice round shape of the curl.

A loop opens into a different plane.

Polishing

Normally, you wait until a project is completed to polish it. With this project, however, it may be easier for you to use the polishing pads on individual links before the bracelet is complicated with charms. Polishing pads should not be used on objects other than metal. Their abrasive nature and/or polishing compounds can damage soft surfaces.

Polishing individual links before it is assembled with charms.

Link as You Go

By making the links separate first, and then linking them together, you are able to visually isolate and examine their individual shapes. Are you happy with what you've made? Do they look symmetrical? Do they look like horseshoes? Does the chain move freely or get hung up and snag? Once you are happy with their forms, and confident that you can repeat the process, move on to forming and linking them as you go.

To assemble the first and second links, begin by laying them both on their backs and heading in the same direction. Overlap the second ring on top of the first. Slide (pop in) the second link into the first link's open curls. Use your needle-nose chain pliers to grab and rotate the curls back into their original position, i.e. close the doors.

Use your needle-nose chain pliers to make adjustments and completely close the curled link. Check for movement. If jewelry doesn't flow freely, it will grind, work harden, and eventually break because of the stress. If you tweak the connections, make a mental note on how to improve on the next link.

2. Use your needle-nose chain pliers to make adjustments and completely close the curled link.

3. The linked horseshoes should articulate/move freely after they are connected.

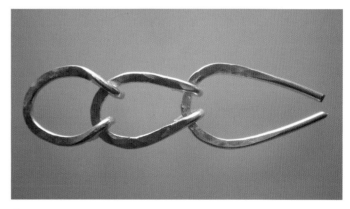

4. To form and link as you go, insert a new horseshoe chain link after it's been hammered but before you curl up the ends.

1. Assemble the first and second links by laying them on their backs, overlapping. Slide the second link into the first link's open curls.

The title of this particular bracelet is "Canadian Influence." It tells a story of three women (hi Janet, Jann and Debra!) who flew down from Chilliwack, British Columbia to take a week's worth of private lessons from me. We had a fantastic time exchanging funny stories, great music, and charms.

Horseshoe Chain Clasp

To make a simple wire hook for the end of your chain, begin by cutting 4 inches of the same gauge wire that you used for the links.

Use your needle-nose chain pliers to grab and hold onto the wire and the rosary pliers to form the rounded shapes.

Follow the progression of photographic steps, and keep in mind that with practice, you will become efficient and confident. The goal is not to have your final piece look chewed up and tortured.

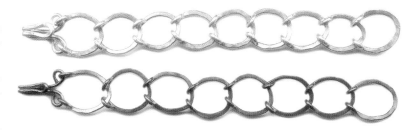

A simple wire hook ends the horseshoe chain.

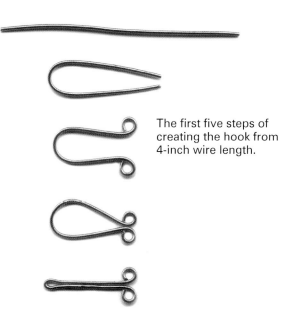

The first five steps of creating the hook from 4-inch wire length.

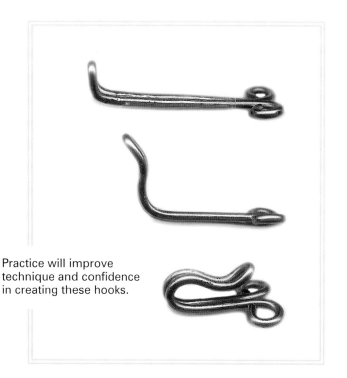

Practice will improve technique and confidence in creating these hooks.

Briolette Wrap

Harnessing Found Objects

A simple way of permanently capturing objects with wire is the briolette wrap. It involves winding wire through an object, then coiling the wire into a closed loop on top. A briolette is a (gem) stone that is teardrop shaped and flattened so it has a front and back. The hole can be oriented from side to side or front to back. The briolette wrap can also be used on found objects as well as beads, as long as it has a hole.

What makes a professional briolette wrap? Following are some pointers:

- The coiled neck is short and strong rather than long and spindly.
- The end of the wire is tucked so that it doesn't get snagged in clothing or hair and unwind.
- The coil should be consistent, compact and neat in appearance.
- The finished piece must dangle freely. If it doesn't, repeated incidents of getting stuck will work harden the metal and cause it to break.
- If connected to a necklace chain, the briolette wrap should be big enough to allow the pendant to slide freely on the chain, while small enough not to slip over the clasp ends and fall off.

Practice makes perfect! Don't be discouraged if at first you don't succeed. While the briolette wrap technique is consistent with predictable shapes such as the briolette, you may have to modify your technique when using it on uniquely individual found objects.

Choosing Wire

After you've selected what you are going to briolette wrap, test different gauges of wire to see which one fits comfortably. You want to use the thickest that will fit into the hole without force. If the wire flexes and is too tight, it may break the object.

Cut a workable length of wire off of your spool or coil: not so short that it won't be enough, and not so much that you get tangled in it or poke your couch cat in the eye. For me, it's around seven inches of wire. Feed the wire through the bead/found object. Leave approximately an inch sticking out of one side of the object.

Tools Checklist
- Flush cutter
- Gauge
- Glasses
- Needle-nose chain pliers
- Rosary pliers
- Ruler

Materials Checklist
- Found objects and/or beads
- Wire in a gauge that comfortably fits the objects/beads

Find the thickest gauge of wire that will fit without force into the hole of your found object.

Centering the Wire

Using your thumb and index finger, pinch both ends of the wire up directly above the bead/object. Use your needle-nose chain pliers to press the wires side by side. Note that one leg of the wire is shorter than the other. The length of the shorter wire determines how long the neck of the briolette wrap will be. Use your flush cutters to trim the shorter wire to approximately 1/8 inch.

Pinch both ends of the wire up directly above the bead/object.

Use needle-nose chain pliers to press the wires side by side.

Use flush cutters to trim the shorter wire to approximately 1/8 inch.

Making the Neck and Head

Use your needle-nose chain pliers to bend the longer wire into a right angle. The bend has to be flush (even) with the tip of the shorter wire.

Study the orientation of the hole in your bead/object. Is it left to right or front to back? To photograph the steps, I made the loop in the same plane as the flattened briolette. Great for photos, but if I were to wear it on a chain, it would hang sideways. Adjust your plane accordingly.

Use the rosary pliers to form a complete loop that will sit, like a head, squarely on top of the neck.

Use needle-nose chain pliers to bend the longer wire into a right angle, even with the tip of the shorter wire.

Use the rosary pliers to form a complete loop that will sit, like a head, squarely on top of the neck.

Holding the loop firmly with the needle-nose chain pliers, wind the wire into an even, tight coil around the neck.

Wrapping the Coil Around the Neck

Once you've finished forming a nice round head that sits symmetrically on top of the neck, hold it firmly with the needle-nose chain pliers. Wind the wire into an even, tight coil around the neck.

Finishing the End

When do you stop coiling? Just in time to tuck in and hide the end of the wire. If the end of the sharp wire sticks out, it will get caught and scratch the wearer.

Use the flush cutters to trim the end of the wire and the tips of the needle-nose chain pliers to tuck the end in. Feel your work with your fingers to ensure it's not sharp.

Matchsticks and Torches

Tier Necklace

I developed this workshop to introduce beginning students to butane torches, fire safety, and give them an opportunity explore how fine silver behaves when exposed to heat. Over the years, we've played with variations on how to connect the matchstick shapes. The Full- and Half- Tier designs are popular with students of all levels. Depending on your temperament, the most challenging (or relaxing) part of this project is the repetition.

The instruction focuses on the Full-Tier version in which the hanging matchsticks end in a V-formation. By contrast, the Half-Tier contains half of the V-tiers which mirror each other on the left and right half of the necklace.

The Matchsticks and Torches Half-Tier Necklace contains within it several design possibilities. For a crisp look, the dangles are oriented so they close in the front. Compare this too the Full-Tier version, where the hanging matchsticks close in back.

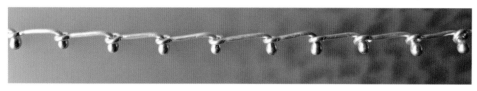

The base chain for the Tier Necklace is composed of single matchsticks with their heads bent at right angles. How long the links need to be depends on how many hanging matchsticks you attach to them. If you decide to wear the base chain by itself, I recommend cutting 1 1/8-inch links after you draw the bead (ball up wire).

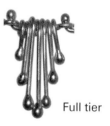

Full tier

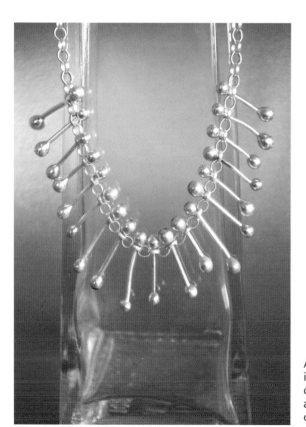

Tools Checklist
- Butane torch
- Cookie tray
- Flush cutters
- Gauge
- Glasses
- Long cross-lock tweezers
- Metal ruler
- Needle-nose chain pliers
- Rosary pliers
- Scrap jar
- Tripods with screens

Materials Checklist
- Butane
- Tumbler
- 16-gauge fine silver wire

After you've gotten comfortable with making matchsticks try experimenting with manufactured chain. Use a thin-gauge wire that fits loosely in a chain link after drawing the first bead. Be sure to use your tweezers tips as a heat sink so the chain stays cool (and tarnish free) as you ball up the other end of the matchstick.

Playing With Fire

We were all taught at an early age not to play with fire. As an adult, you now know that we can have fun with fire if we observe two simple rules: don't set anything on fire and don't burn yourself!

Cookie Sheet

Find a stable table to place your cookie sheet. Remove any flammable (or melt-able) items from the vicinity. Remember that, besides not torching the cookie sheet itself, you have to be conscious about not overshooting your project and thus torching the area behind or beside the sheet.

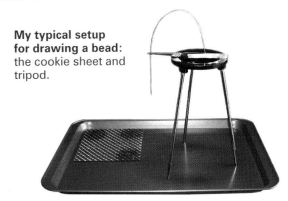

My typical setup for drawing a bead: the cookie sheet and tripod.

Tripod

Place the tripod on the baking sheet, away from the edges. For this project, lay the wire mesh in a corner of your tray. This will provide a place for the matchsticks to air cool. Quenching fine silver right after it is molten causes thermal shock, which in turn creates stress-related micro-cracks in its re-crystallization process. These cracks weaken the structure of your final piece and could cause problems in the future such as breaking.

Preparing the Wire

Cut a manageable piece (about 1 foot) of 16-gauge wire. Use the locking tweezers to suspend one end of the wire from the tripod. Make sure that end is pointed straight down so when you draw a bead (ball up wire), the result won't be crooked. If the bead drips, it needs to land, splat, scatter, and/or roll in the tray not in your lap.

Stabilize the opposite end of the wire by bending and tucking it into the back of the tweezers. This will keep it out of the way while you work. As the wire shortens, bend it in various ways to keep the tweezers-and-wire unit from flipping (rotating).

Note the ends of the wire: one pointed straight down, while the other is held in place by tension.

Concept: Heat Sinks

When setting up projects to work with heat, the concept of heat sinks is an important part of your strategy. Remember waterbeds? If you've ever used one, you may have found yourself sleeping on it after the water heater broke. The result was that no matter how many layers of blankets you put on top of yourself, you spent the night freezing. The reason why was because the water in the mattress had more mass than your body, so it won in terms of temperature exchange.

A more updated version of this scenario is the air mattress. You know, the kind that inflates with a vacuum cleaner? Because of its motor, the air in the vacuum cleaner is warm, so nothing will seem amiss until around 2:00 A.M., when you wake up cold. The floor pulled the heat out of the mattress, which pulled the heat out of all the contact areas of your body. At that point, you will vow to never sleep on an air mattress again, unless it has twelve quilts separating you from the heat sink.

Hypothermia is what we call it if you end up stranded in cold water. No matter how hard your body works, it can't overcome the cooler mass around you.

When I went on a three-day wilderness kayak in British Columbia, August 2003, my biggest safety concern dealt with the potential hazard of falling into the extremely cold waters of the Johnston Straight. The heat sink effect from these waters can cause hypothermia within ten minutes.

In jewelry, it is helpful to be conscious and strategize when working with heat sinks. For example, when setting up your tripod, cross-lock tweezers, and wire, you'll want minimum contact between all of them in terms of mass, so that you can heat the wire up faster.

Use the very tips of the cross-lock tweezers to hold your wire, as opposed to further down, where the tweezers are larger (and more mass or contact area). The tripod's top is made of a cast-metal ring. This can be a huge heat sink. To help counteract heat transference, cantilever the cross-lock tweezers out as far as you can without them falling. That will create more distance between the tip of the wire that you want to melt and ball up, and the heat sink of the tripod's cast ring platform.

Drawing a Bead

Before drawing a bead, identify the focal point of the torch flame: the tip of the bright blue cone. That is the hottest spot. This means you can be too far away *and* too close to your piece.

If you have trouble with depth perception, listen to your flame. If you are too close, it makes a harsh sound. When I can't see the tip of the bright blue cone, I listen for that harsh sound and then pull back slightly to find the focal point. To prove to my students that this method works (and help someone who had eye surgery and no depth perception), I demonstrated that I could successfully draw a bead with my eyes closed by just using sound. No kidding.

Heat the wire from the bottom up. Make sure your flame is aimed horizontally (and parallel to the table) or upward. Of course, keep your hand and torch out of the way in case a bead of molten metal drips off. Don't aim the flame down on the wire, because you may overshoot it and torch the table. You might also melt a neck into the matchstick, causing it to drip.

Make the matchstick as large as possible. Once you get the hang of it, you'll be able to predict when to stop heating by the behavior of the metal as it balls up. I find there is a slight pause in the plumping up of the bead right before it's overcome by gravity and falls off. Lay the wire on the mesh to cool.

While your first piece is cooling, cut another working piece of wire and make another matchstick. As you create more matchsticks, your working wire will shorten. Eventually, you can flip the tweezers to work on the opposite end of the wire without risking torching the pan or branding yourself.

1. The focal point, the hottest spot, of the torch flame is the tip of the bright blue cone.

2. Make sure your flame is aimed horizontally (and parallel to the table) or upward. Don't aim down on the wire, because you may overshoot it and torch the table.

3. New matchsticks cool on wire mesh.

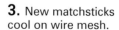

4. Cut a 3-inch matchstick after drawing the bead.

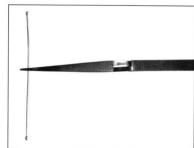

Making the Matchstick Wire Hook

The best way to begin the matchstick necklace is with the matchstick hook. The first part of the hook design looks like a Shepherd's crook. Study the steps depicted in the photographs to see the progression of how the hook is formed, and look ahead in the lesson to see how it's attached to the first matchstick base chain link. This simple hook can be used in lots of other styles of necklaces and bracelets. The matchstick eye (hook partner) is the last step in making the matchstick necklace.

Forming the Shepherd's Crook/Hook

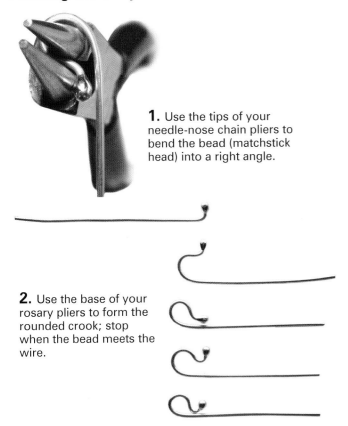

1. Use the tips of your needle-nose chain pliers to bend the bead (matchstick head) into a right angle.

2. Use the base of your rosary pliers to form the rounded crook; stop when the bead meets the wire.

Adding a Closed Coil to the Crook/Hook

1. Bend the wire into a right angle, away from the crook. Note that you may have to open the crook a little to use your tool.

Adding a closed coil to the crook/hook.

2. Starting at the wire's right angle, use your rosary pliers to form a complete circle.
3. Test the complete circle to make sure it is *large* enough to hold a 16-gauge piece of wire.
4. Test it again to make sure it is *small* enough to seat a 16-gauge matchstick head without falling through.
5. Hold the circle in place with the needle-nose chain pliers, while:
6. Closing the loop by wrapping the wire into a nice neat coil (approximately three coils deep).
7. Study the plane of the hook. Note that in the finished matchstick hook, the loop is perpendicular to the hook. Use your hands to adjust the plane.

You'll want to trim off excess wire using your flush cutters, but before you do, arrange the ending so it is on the inside of the design rather than the back or sides. The wire's tip will be sharp and can snag clothing and scratch skin if it is on the outside of the design.

Grading & Assembling the Hanging Matchsticks

Decide whether you want to make half-tier (four hanging matchsticks) or a full-tier unit (seven hanging matchsticks). In both cases, the longest matchstick is cut at 1 1/4 inch in length including the bead. Begin with cutting it first. Use your rosary pliers to curl up the end. Squeeze it completely closed. The secret to making the hanging matchsticks is that they are measured 1/4 inch apart in length, after you've drawn the bead. Organize the tiers by laying them out in graduated sizes.

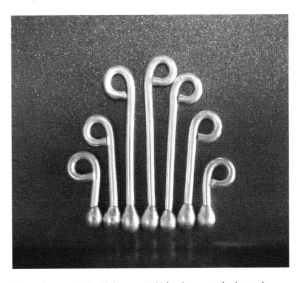

Hanging matchsticks are 1/4 inch apart in length, after the bead is drawn. Organize the tiers by laying them out in graduated sizes.

Matchstick Chain Link

You'll need something to
hang your matchsticks
from. The base chain link is

also a 16-gauge, 1 1/4 inch matchstick. Bend its head into
a right angle. Turn the clasp hook downward, then feed
the first matchstick link through its loop from top down.

Add the Hanging Matchsticks

Slide the hanging matchsticks onto the base
chain. Double check that the formation looks the
way you intended. Rearrange or trim hanging
matchsticks if necessary. Pay particular attention to
which way you are hanging the matchsticks; there
is a front and back to the design.

The hanging
matchsticks begin
close to the hook
to visually integrate
form and function.

Use your rosary pliers to curl up the end of the base
chain link when you are finished. This will serve as the
closed loop that seats the next base chain link.

Bird's eye (isolated) view of
a Full Matchstick unit with 7
hanging matchsticks.

Finishing with the Matchstick Wire Eye

The end of the neck-
lace has a simple match-
stick "eye" that provides
someplace for the hook
to, well uh, hook into.

1. Cut a 3-inch matchstick including the bead.
2. Use the tips of your needle-nose chain pliers to
   bend the head of your 3-inch matchstick into a
   right angle.
3. Add the final tier of hanging matchsticks.
4. Use the base of your rosary pliers to form a
   complete loop. Test its size: It has to be large
   enough to hold the matchstick hook.
5. Wrap the end of the wire into a nice, neat coil.
6. Check the plane of the loop.
7. Arrange for the coil to end on the underside (as
   opposed to the top or sides), so that it won't get
   caught in clothing or scratch skin.
8. Use your flush cutters to trim off any excess
   wire.
9. Use the tips of your needle-nose chain pliers to
   tuck or press the end of the wire flat if necessary.

Completed
Full-Tier version

Jump Rings

Preparation for Fusing Loops

It may not look like much, but the jump ring is an essential tool in jewelry design. It is the link that connects most pendants to their chain. It offers movement, transition, and protection between the chain and its clasp.

A jump ring, made correctly, is strong and flush (smooth at the join) while still being able to open in case of an emergency. Under normal conditions it should wear well – not scratch the skin or get caught in fabric, your hair, your pet's hair, etc. A jump ring, by definition, is not permanently closed. To do so, you'd need to either use a jewelry welder, soldering, or fusing techniques. Permanently closed jump rings are referred to as soldered (or fused) rings to avoid confusion.

When I learned how to make jump rings in college, we used a jeweler's saw blade to cut the coil. It was an awkward technique for me, which I wasn't fond of. It wasn't until I began teaching workshops at The Magical Trinket in the San Francisco Bay Area during the late 1990s that I was introduced to flush cutter method by the owner, Eve Blake. With a little practice and a lot of awareness, this technique is easy and only uses a few tools: two sets of needle-nose chain pliers plus a flush cutter. How liberating it is to be able to quickly and easily make a jump ring (or loop for fusing) without a jeweler's saw and bench pin.

Preparing the Wire

Measure out approximately six inches of wire. By working with a smaller length, you will reduce the work hardening that occurs with coiling. Why is that important? Work hardening makes the metal springier as you coil. This in turn makes the wire less able to hug the dowel. The result is jump rings that get progressively larger as you coil.

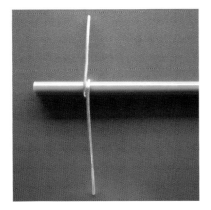

Begin wrapping jump wrings in the center of wire.

Tools Checklist
- Dowel rods; experiment with 3/8, 1/2, and 5/8 inch sizes
- Flush cutters
- Gauge
- Scrap jar
- Two needle-nose chain pliers

Materials Checklist
Wire: experiment with 16-gauge and 14-gauge fine silver

Coiling

To further cut the work hardening, rather than coiling from the end of the wire, we will begin coiling from the middle of the wire, out. This cuts the work hardening in half! The coil should be perpendicular (straight) onto the dowel. Control the wire so the coil is nice and neat without gaps. When you are finished, use your needle-nose chain pliers to press the ends of the wire down onto the dowel rod. This way, you've ended the wire "in the round" and made use of as much wire as possible. Put the end of the dowel on your table and push the coil down as far as possible, then use your hands to get it off the rest of the way.

Wrapped and removed from dowel.

Flush Cutting

Use the tip of your flush cutters to pull the first complete loop away from the coil. Angle the cutters so when you make your cut, it will be at a right angle, not diagonal, to the wire.

After you've cut each loop from the coil, examine the jump rings. One end will have a sharp, pinched cut. That corresponds to the valley side of the flush cutter. The other end of the wire should be a blunt, right-angle cut, which corresponds to the flush side of the cutters.

Use the flush side of your cutter to trim off the pinches on each loop, and be sure to do so at a right angle. What makes the jump rings flush when they are closed is the meeting of two right angles into a flush join. Don't forget to save your fine silver scraps.

Concept: Closing vs. Over Closing

I prefer to use two needle-nose chain pliers to close my jump rings; one to hold the ring in its base, and the other to close the loop. For regular jump rings, you need only wiggle the ends back and forth while pressing the loop closed. Feel and listen to the ends scraping to make sure the jump ring is really closed. To prepare a loop for fusing, however, the jump rings should be over closed.

You began with dead soft wire; however, coiling caused it to work harden. If you close the loops like a jump ring, they will probably open up as you heat them for fusing. This is because on your way to the temperatures needed for fusing, you go through an annealing phase – when the metal has a dull orange glow. Annealing relaxes metal from its hardened state back to a dead soft state.

To prevent the loop from relaxing so much that it opens, we create a spring-like tension by over closing the loop. Even though it will still relax as it becomes annealed, the additional spring-like tension will keep it closed.

To over close, use your fingers and/or the chain pliers to push the ends of the wire past each other on both sides; in other words, pretend they are kissing each other on both cheeks like many European people do! A couple of times on each cheek should do it. Then line up the ends so the loop is tension set and closed. Make sure that it is really flush (no gap) and closed without a step. Successful fusing depends on good, flush contact.

This jump ring illustrates both what flush cuts look like and the concept of over closing a ring to create a spring. The tension keeps it closed when heated.

Three examples of jump rings. The left one has a pinched and flush cut, which is typical after cutting the coil apart. The center ring has been trimmed so there are two flush cuts. On the right, after it has been over closed, the jump ring is tension set for fusing. Note the flush join.

Fusing Loops

In the classroom and in my distance-learning lessons, I begin with teaching students how to fuse a simple fine silver jump ring permanently closed. Fused loops can be shaped, hammered, textured, and cold-connected to become components, pendants, and stackable rings. Fused loops are the foundation for many of the fusing projects that I developed. No matter what type of fusing project you focus on, the basic tools and materials are the same. With this and all projects, read the whole process before beginning.

A bridge will freeze before the road because it is thinner in mass than the road/land around it. That makes it more vulnerable to cold. In fusing, if part of your project is straddling/bridging a hole, that spot will heat up faster than the rest of the project and melt down.

Placement: Lots o' Loops

Find a safe place to play with fire. Gently place your soft kiln brick on the cookie sheet. Stagger the loops on the smooth side of the brick. This will help prevent you from melting the ones in the back while working on the ones in the front. The join on each loop should be at a six o'clock position, so you don't have to hunt for them. This also allows you to repeat the same physical movements over and over as you fuse lots of loops. Leave a margin around the edge of your brick, just in case the torch overshoots.

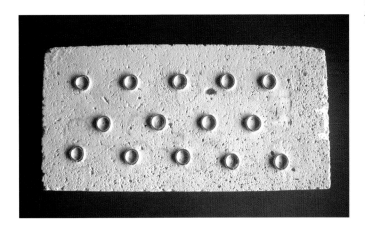

Stagger the loops on the smooth side of the brick, the join on each loop at a six o'clock position.

Basic Fusing Tools Checklist
- Butane torch
- Combination forming/planishing hammer (optional)
- Cookie tray
- Dowel rods (3/8 inch suggested for this project, but experiment with other sizes)
- Flush cutters
- Gauge
- Glasses
- Long cross-lock tweezers
- Mouse pad
- Needle-nose chain pliers
- Rosary pliers
- Scrap jar
- Soft kiln brick
- Steel block (if hammering)
- Tumbler (if polishing or hardening)

Basic Fusing Materials Checklist
- Butane
- Chewing gum
- Dawn® liquid soap (if using tumbler)
- 14-gauge fine silver wire
- Polishing pads

Fire Strategy

Once you understand the behavior of fire, you can manipulate it. Here are some of my rules on fire and fusing.

- You can't fuse what doesn't have good contact. Metal won't jump to the other side of a gap. That's why the loops have to be flush-closed.
- The more surface area of the butt join that is touching, the more likely it is to fuse smoothly. Yes, it's really called a butt join because the ends are butted up against each other. No joking.
- Always preheat your piece by heating the brick (not the loop) around, inside and below the join of the loop.
- Putting direct heat onto a join will only cause you to draw (ball up) two beads!
- Don't forget, the bridge freezes before the road. In our case, a bridge is the metal strad-

dling a hole in the brick. Since the rest of the loop has a heat sink (the brick) and the part of the loop that is straddling the hole does not, that spot will heat up quicker and melt down before the rest of the loop is affected. In short: avoid holes!

- Molten metal travels to the hottest spot. This defies gravity. Repeat this ten times and remember it when wondering why you have a lump somewhere on your ring.
- Think of the brick as your pizza stone that bakes the pizza from underneath and more evenly, even with heat coming from above.
- Don't set anything on fire.
- When you pull the heat away, don't aim the torch at the Teflon, table, cat, drapery, wallpaper, well meaning onlookers, etc.

Lighting

The ideal studio for fusing has controllable lighting: bright light to make and check the join, and twilight to watch the color of the metal as you fuse. If you don't have ideal lighting, you may have to use a magnification visor.

Test Your Torch

You'll want to make sure that you know how to turn your torch on and off and how to adjust the flame before you start. Since there are many sizes of butane torches, I can't suggest a low, medium, or high flame. Keep in mind, a full torch is more powerful than one that is half empty.

Flame Focus

Angle (rotate) the cookie sheet and brick a little so you can see the flame from the side and heat your loop symmetrically on both sides of the join. If you are right-handed, pivot your cookie sheet (with brick) to the right so your torch approaches the join head-on. I've rotated my brick to the right in order to fuse and photograph the steps. Even though the 6 o'clock position has shifted, I will continue to refer to it as a 6 o'clock position. Left-handed? Rotate the tray to the left.

Approach your loop by preheating the brick below the 6:00 position of the join.

The soft kiln brick is a great refractory tool. That means it's great at reflecting heat back, rather than being a heat sink. By heating it (rather than the loop), you are also heating the loop evenly and from underneath. This will ensure that the join is fused all the way through.

Preheating the Brick

Begin preheating the brick below the 6 o'clock position. When the brick turns orange, sweep the flame around the outside of the loop (on the brick) and maintain the same (orange) level of heat. Briefly dip into the middle of the loop to heat the brick there as well.

Fusing Loops

As the loop begins to heat (as a result of heating the brick around it), you'll notice it turning dull orange. This is the annealing phase of the heating process, and if the loop was properly over closed, it should have enough tension to remain closed. However, if it relaxes so much that the join opens, you'll have to move on to the next loop (and work on your "over closing" skills).

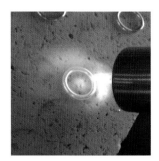

Go around the outside of the loop, focusing on heating the brick. Avoid directly heating the metal.

It is possible to trim failed loops to make a new butt join and try again. The trick is to trim off any uneven metal so you have a good, clean contact. Since you've got nothing to lose, try it! The experience will help you hone your fire manipulation skills. If all else fails, melt down the loop to a grain of metal to be used as decorative accents or granulation.

Mantra: Swish, Down, Pause

Once the fine silver reaches the dull orange glow, begin concentrating on the area between 3 and 9 o'clock. When the fine silver reaches the flash point (looks wet and begins melting), you have to lead it to where you need it, which is directly *below* the 6 o'clock join on the brick.

Repeatedly sweep the torch flame from the 3 to the 9 o'clock positions, then pause below the 6 join to make *that* the hottest spot on the brick. Study the loop's reaction carefully as you repeat the sweep-

and-pause technique. The loop will appear frosty as it begins to "sweat." Once the "sweat beads" of molten metal merge, it will travel toward the hottest spot. If only one side of the join gets wet, you are not heating both sides evenly. Change the angle of your torch slightly to get a more symmetrical effect.

Keep reminding yourself that you are heating the brick, and the brick is heating your loop. By continually swishing between the 3 and 9 o'clock positions, then pausing/heating below the 6 o'clock position of the join, you are coaxing the metal to flow toward the join. The brick underneath the join will also draw the metal down through the join, thus ensuring that your loop is fused all the way through.

As both sides of the join become evenly wet, capillary action will fuse them together. Part of the fusing process is knowing when to stop. Lingering to admire your work will cause a lumpy bumpy mess or meltdown. With practice, you'll learn how to psychoanalyze fire and control it!

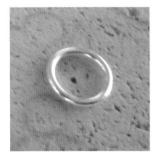

Once the fine silver reaches the dull orange glow, begin concentrating on the area between 3 and 9 o'clock.

Checking the Loops

You shouldn't see a straight line where you fused. You may, however, see an indentation or impression. As you get better, the loops will look smoother and more even in mass distribution. That's your goal!

Place the tip of your tweezers on the edge of you loop and flip (roll) it over to check the backside. This is faster than picking them up individually and potentially burning yourself. If you see a defined line where the join was, you'll have to refuse it. If the ends of the wire melted (began drawing into beads), you'll have to flush cut and over close them again to try refusing.

For loops that are slightly lumpy and bumpy, I set them aside to hammer. The textures are a great distraction from uneven shapes. If the loops are hopeless in terms of structural integrity, either melt them down into grains to fuse onto future projects, or toss them into your fine silver scrap jar. Lumps in your loops reveal the hot spots. Since the extra metal had to come from somewhere, you will probably notice the complementary thin spot.

If your loop melted down at the join, it either wasn't flush cut well, or you put too much direct heat on it. Remember to heat the brick, not the loop, and coax the wet metal toward the flame when it reaches the flash point.

Do not quench your fine silver loops! When molten fine silver begins to cool, its matrix (crystalline structure) needs to reform naturally. Quenching it during this process creates thermal shock, which interrupts this re-growth with micro-cracks. This in turn creates inconsistencies in the metal, making it weak. If the piece is stressed, in the future it may crack along those lines. Instead, stack the loops in a corner of your brick and allow them to air cool. It won't take long.

Loopy Fun

There are a lot of great things you can do with fused loops. Classical and contemporary recipes for loop-in-loop chains are almost infinite in variation, and you can find them all over the web.

Hammer your fine silver loops on the steel block to create interesting textures. Scout hardware, kitchen, and thrift stores to look for steel or hardened brass objects. Lay them on top of your loop and use a regular household claw hammer to transfer the design or pattern. Save the pristine planishing/forming hammer for direct results such as stretching and dappling the fine silver. Using your needle-nose chain pliers, bite the loops into edgy geometric shapes. The rosary pliers are great for softer, rounded shapes.

Lumpy loops serve as interesting, irregular surfaces that are perfect for hammering. If, however, you have a thin spot, it will most likely break.

Add jump rings to the fused loops and connect them to ear wires, turn them into pendants or link them up into a chain. Different dowel rod sizes create different jump rings, so you can play with them as well. See what happens if you double and triple the jump rings. There's no end to all the variations you can come up with. Mostly, experiment and have a lot of fun torching and hammering.

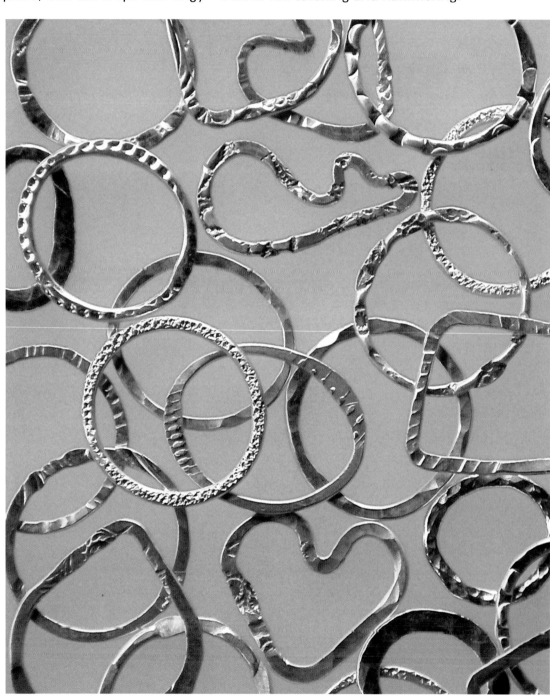

All of these loops were fused round first, then shaped and/or hammered on a steel block. Once you "become one with" your rosary and needle-nose chain pliers, you can easily make simple cookie-cutter-type shapes. I'm sure you already spotted the heart, but did you see the whale in this photo?

Saturn Links

I've spent many hours fusing loops both in and out of the classroom. While I teach, there is usually a time close to the end of the workshop when students are in their groove and working to perfect their skills. That's when I have an opportunity to experiment with variations on our project. The Saturn Link design was derived from my Fused Loops and Stackable Rings fusing workshop.

Making Grains

After melting inferior loops into grains, I use AA tweezers to nestle them carefully inside a successfully fused loop of the same mass. The curvature of the loop hugs the curvature of the fine silver grain, creating the contact needed for fusing.

Because the loop and grain are the same mass, they should heat up at the same rate, right? Wrong. The difference is not the mass, but how it is distributed. A loop is a thin, spread-out shape. A grain is a dense mass that covers very little surface area of the brick. In order to fuse them together, they have to be the same temperature at the same time, meaning they have to reach the flash point at the same time. The compact shape of the grain will need slightly more (heat) attention. In fact, it goes one step further: The heat from the grain will overcome and attract the loop to it if the brick underneath is hot enough to allow the metal to flow. Orient the grain inside the loop at the 6 o'clock position.

The Saturn Link design is a great way to practice fusing shapes that are the same mass but distributed differently. The trick is to keep the crisp Saturn form while fusing.

Basic Fusing Tools Checklist
Use the basic setup for fusing and add/or substitute the following items:
- AA tweezers
- Butane torch: small to medium size
- 1/4-inch dowel (for fine silver Saturn rings)
- 3/13-inch dowel (for sterling jump rings)
- Fine silver scrap jar
- Sterling silver scrap jar

Basic Fusing Materials Checklist
- 16-gauge fine silver wire (Saturn rings)
- 16-gauge sterling silver (jump rings to cold connect chain)

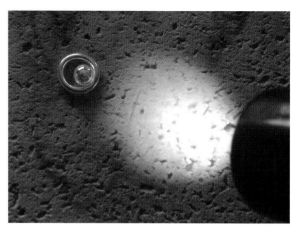

Approach the saturn link from the six o'clock position. The grain needs to be slightly hotter than the ring for a successful fuse.

The goal of this project is to practice fusing items of the same mass (but distributed differently) without losing their form. Just like the fused loops: The more surface area that is touching, the better the fine silver can be drawn along the seam/join by the heat of your flame. To explain exactly how to do this is like explaining exactly how to ride a bicycle: You can present a whole lecture on it, but eventually you just have to get on the bike and fall down a few times to find your balance. In this case, you don't' have to fall down, just melt down a few of your attempts.

A variation in the Saturn Link involves using the needle-nose chain pliers to squeeze the Saturn rings into a peak at the top. Connect the links with jump rings to create a cascade effect.

It's easy to make a fine silver grain! Just use your butane torch to completely melt down a botched loop, right on top of the soft kiln brick.

The Cascading Saturn Link Chain looks great when hanging freely.

Cold connect the fused Saturn links with jump rings.

Art Deco Spiral Chain

Ready for the next challenge? The premise of my Art Deco Chain project is to increase the contact between the surface areas of the wires. The fusing skill you'll focus on is to pull the metal along the seams without degrading the visual and structural integrity of the links. Begin with my recipe, then experiment with thicker and longer pieces of wire. Write down the results of your experiments so you can troubleshoot the links that give you problems and recreate your works of genius. I use a flatbed scanner to photocopy my samples and write notes directly on the copy.

Forming the Rectangular Spiral

Flush cut 18-gauge silver wire into a 4-inch length. You will begin forming the rectangular spiral in the middle of the design. Use your needle-nose chain pliers to bend the first right angle approximately 1/8 inch from the end. Each face of the square is approximately 1/8 inch. It doesn't need to be exact. Butt the wire's flush cut ends up against itself to complete the square, then go from there. Over close the butt join to create tension.

As you work your way around the rectangular spiral, keep the right angles crisp.

1. Use your needle-nose chain pliers to bend the first right angle approximately 1/8 inch from the end. Over close the butt join to create tension.

2. As you work your way around the rectangular spiral, keep the right angles crisp.

Basic Fusing Tools Checklist
Use the basic setup for fusing and making matchsticks. Add/substitute the following items:

Basic Fusing Materials Checklist
- Small manufactured clasp
- Two sterling silver jump rings, at least 18 gauge thick
- 18-gauge fine silver wire

3. The assembly is fused lying flat. The end of the wire that is butted up against itself is fused to make a closed, complete square. The long stretches across the bottom and top are fused by moving the torch flame horizontally back and forth across them until the fine silver follows the heat and fills the seam.

4. A fused link, it's tail ready to be drawn into a bead.

Fusing Elongated Seams

With this and all fusing projects, make sure that your piece is flat. When you lay it on the brick, make sure that it isn't straddling a hole. This helps promote even heating. The brick is your heat helper from underneath. It ensures that your piece will fuse all the way through.

Orient your project so the end of the wire (in the middle square) is aiming toward the 6 o'clock position. Preheat the brick under the 6 o'clock position. Use sweeping gestures to heat the middle of the design and around the outside. Do not allow the heat to linger directly on the metal, or it will melt and draw a bead.

Once your piece has a dull orange glow, sweep the torch flame into the middle of the design. Fuse the end of the wire that is butted up against itself to make a closed, complete square.

Next, fuse the long stretch across the bottom by moving the torch flame horizontally back and forth across it until the fine silver follows the heat and fills the seam.

To fuse the long stretch across the top, begin by preheating the brick around the end of the wire that is jutting out into space. Sweep the heat, on the brick, from the end of the wire toward the design. Once the fine silver turns orange, watch for the flash point, then draw the metal down the seam.

Because this design is more complex compared to the fused loops, you may have to use your torch from different angles. Just be careful not to torch yourself or anything in your workspace beside the brick and fine silver.

Drawing a Bead on the Tail

After you've fused your individual rectangular spiral chain links, pick out the best ones. Use your cross-lock tweezers and tripod to hang the links and draw a bead on the end of the extended wire. The beaded tail will become the coiled link that holds the separate chain links together. The last link does not have a tail.

Use the beaded tail to coil onto the next link and create a hinge. The chain should move freely.

Closing Delicate Designs

When I make lightweight or delicate chains, I opt to buy small manufactured clasps rather than making my own. Some have steel springs to stay closed, which is more secure. Their light weight helps keep them out of sight in the back of the neck. Make one sterling jump ring to attach the clasp to the chain and the other to hook into.

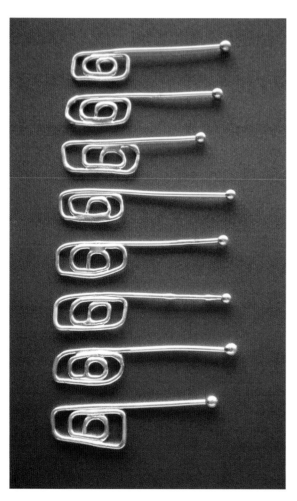

After you've made a bunch of the Art Deco Spiral Chain links, pick out the best and grade them in size. For a necklace, line them up so the biggest and longest links will be in the middle.

Art Nouveau Chain

My Art Nouveau Chain design is similar to the Art Deco in construction and fusing techniques. It has a softer, more organic look due to using the rosary pliers. Each link is a self-contained, closed shape that depends on a jump ring to connect it to its neighbor.

Quick Steps to Form and Fuse

1. Cut the 16-gauge fine silver wire to a 3-inch length.
2. You will begin this design in the middle. Use the tips of the needle nose chain pliers to start a tight spiral at the end of the wire. There shouldn't be any space inside the spiral, so squeeze it closed when you begin forming it.
3. You'll have more leverage to turn the spiral by using the base of the needle-nose chain pliers.
4. The spiral contains 1 1/2 turns.
5. The links are connected by jump rings to make a chain. Note that on one side of the spiral, there is the "handle" to hold the jump ring that connects to the next link. On the opposite side of the spiral, there isn't a handle but instead *room* for the other jump.
6. Use the needle nose chain pliers to build a larger, random shape around the spiral. Be creative and have fun with this part!
7. To fuse the design closed, you will have to make sure the wire doubles up, side by side, to create a horizontal seam.
8. Terminate the design by flush cutting the end of the wire.
9. Butt it up against the design. Over close to ensure this stays closed once the piece heats up and relaxes. This offers a (fused) closed handle for the jump ring to fit into.
10. Hold your link up into the light to make sure the seams and butt join are really touching as much as possible.
11. Also make sure your piece lays flat on the soft kiln brick. This ensures even heating.
12. The fusing steps are basically the same. Preheat the brick in and around your piece first.
13. When the metal turns dull orange, begin focusing on the individual tasks. Fuse the butt join closed first by sweeping across the contact.
14. Draw the metal down the horizontal seam to finish fusing the link closed.

Basic Fusing Tools Checklist

Use the basic setup for fusing and making matchsticks. Add/substitute the following items:
- 1/8-inch dowel rod for jump rings

Basic Fusing Materials Checklist

- Patination supplies
- Pro polish pads
- 16-gauge fine silver for fusing links
- 16-gauge sterling silver for jump rings

Finishing

1. Use the 1/8-inch dowel rod to form the jump rings.
2. Hook your links together.
3. To form a flat, closed coil wire hook, review the Shepherd's Hook/Crook instructions. Instead of drawing a bead, this time you will tightly spiral the end of the wire.
4. Attach the flat closed coil wire hook directly to the last Art Nouveau chain link.
5. If you think the piece is too soft, tumble to harden it.
6. Use your favorite patination method to antique the chain.
7. Pro Polish Pads are a great way to highlight the fine silver.

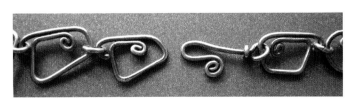

Hugs & Kisses

Original Design

I developed the idea for my Hugs and Kisses Series while teaching on Oahu in 2004. Kailua is on the rainy side of the island and I spent my days off playing with all the tools and materials I'd hauled across the Pacific Ocean with me. This series was the first and larger offspring from the Saturn Links. It also leads the way to more intricate challenges and adventures with fusing.

When experimenting with new ideas, I usually give myself a set of parameters. In the case of the Original Hugs and Kisses series, I wanted to focus on developing a wire design where all the cells were the same gauge and formed on the same-sized dowel. After fusing the loops closed, I limited myself to two basic shapes: round and oval. Then I experimented with different ways to fuse them into individual units. I also wanted the freedom to link the units in all four directions. Once I got the hang of making these, the repetition proved to be relaxing and worthy of a day off.

The pattern reminded me of the symbolic representation for hugs (O) and kisses (X). My technique of hugging (the parts to be fused) and kissing (hard on the brick, sweeping air kisses on the seams) also became a metaphor for describing my technique to a classroom full of students.

Of course, there will always be meltdowns and inferior loops. What a perfect opportunity to turn lemons into lemonade! The center of the Hugs and Kisses link is just asking for the added punctuation of a fused grain detail.

Notes

Nothing new! This design uses the same basic fusing steps. Because it is a larger design, you may want to use a larger butane torch. As always, make sure the cells are flat, not straddling a hole in the brick, hugging each other as much as possible. Preheat the brick around and under the design and then use the sweeping air kisses from all directions to draw the metal where you want.

When I first starting making these, I would fuse all the hugs and kisses at once, then add the grain to the center for a second round of fusing. These days, I'm able to do it all at the same time once I'm warmed up. Viva la kisses!

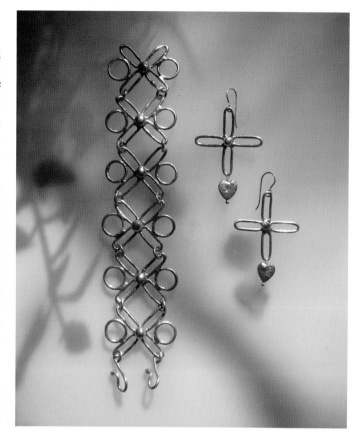

Developed in 2004, my Original Hugs and Kisses project/workshop paved the way for more challenging and satisfying fusing adventures.

Basic Fusing Tools Checklist
Use the basic setup for fusing. Add/substitute the following:
- Mallet (to flatten the XO units)
- Steel block (use with mallet)
- 3/8-inch dowel rod for fused loops
- 3/16-inch dowel rod for jump rings
- Two needle-nose chain pliers

Basic Fusing Materials Checklist
16-gauge fine silver wire

1. A fused loop is elongated

2. Four elongated loops, two round loops, and a grain are fused for Hugs & Kisses.

3. The chain is assembled.

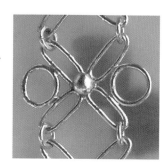

Hugs & Kisses

Daisy & Lotus Blossom

In 2007, Jamie, co-owner of The Bead Gallery on Oahu, invited me to teach my Hugs & Kisses project, but requested that I modify the design into a five-petal flower no more than 1 1/2 inches across. After lots of experimentation I was able to shrink the design down, and my Daisy version was born. It premiered on their website in the spring of 2008 for an upcoming workshop and remained on display for over a year.

As usual, I like to play with variations after my class gets the hang of it. Jason (Jamie's husband) handed me a 14mm Swarovski Rivoli crystal. Using it, plus simple folding and slotting techniques, I developed a layered version called the Lotus Blossom.

Basic Fusing Tools Checklist
Use the basic setup for fusing. Add/substitute the following:
- AA tweezers
- Dowel rod (3/8 inch for small petals)
- Two needle-nose chain pliers

Basic Fusing Materials Checklist
- 16-gauge fine silver
- 14mm cabochons or Swarovski Rivoli crystals (1 per flower)

Quick Steps to Make the Hugs & Kisses: Daisy and Lotus Blossom

You'll have to make a daisy on your way to building the lotus blossom and later, the passion flower.

Lotus Blossom

Fusing/Forming the Star and Daisy

1. Using 16-gauge silver and a 3/8 inch dowel rod, make six jump rings and fuse five of them closed.
2. Stretch five into ovals with your rosary pliers. Save one to make a grain that will be seated in the center of the daisy.
3. Lay them out in a star formation on your soft kiln brick.
4. Make sure they are touching as much as possible in the middle.
5. Tack fuse them together just enough so they hold.
6. On a flat surface such as your cookie sheet, use the tips of your needle-nose pliers to expand the center of each daisy petal.
7. After you've expanded each petal so that it meets its neighbor, pick up the daisy and expand the petals some more until all the gaps are filled.
8. Use your chain pliers to give an extra squeeze in areas that need help.
9. If you find that squeezing one set of petal neighbors opens up the adjacent neighbors, go back

and expand them more using the rosary pliers on a flat surface. You can also use two chain pliers: one to squeeze and the other to hold adjacent cells closed.

10. If your flower is torqued, gently flatten it with the mallet on a steel block.
11. Fuse the petals together.

Stretch five jump rings into ovals with rosary pliers.

Lay them out in a star formation on your soft kiln brick.
Make sure they are touching as much as possible in the middle. Tack fuse them together just enough so they hold.

On a flat surface, use needle-nose pliers to expand the center of each star's rays so they meet their neighbors.

Far left:
Use chain pliers to give an extra squeeze in areas that need help.

Left:
Fuse the star's rays side by side to become a daisy.

The daisy pendant is a great component to hang things from. You can also jump ring several together to make a daisy chain. Use the combination planishing/forming hammer to hide a multitude of imperfections and inconsistencies. Keep in mind, however, that the visual characteristic of fusing is a natural, organic look.

Nobody is perfect, including me. When things go wrong, such as a petal melting down in the last step, I allow the piece to tell me what it wants to be. By allowing the materials and process to speak to me, I avoid a lot of frustration and constantly embark on a creative journey. In this case, I cut out the melted petal and hung a brand new one in its place. The delicate manufactured chain reminded me of wispy spider's threads that capture a passing petal or leaf. If there is a space beside the fused grain in the center of the daisy, I use it to sew on a Swarovski crystal with a thin-gauge fine silver head pin. Repeating a crystal here and there makes the choice look deliberate and confident. Open yourself to hear your muse. Viva la confidence!

Assembling the Lotus Blossom

You will need one five-pointed star and one five-pointed daisy (without the grain in the middle).

1. Use the combination planishing/forming hammer to texture the daisy. Lay it down, textured side up.
2. While firmly holding the center of the star (keep the petals from breaking off at the fused points), use your rosary pliers to gently curl up the ends.
3. Adjust the star petals so they fit into the daisy petals from the back. The two shapes will be interlocked and held by tension after the rivoli or cabochon is set.
4. Lay the rivoli or cabochon in the middle.
5. Hold the assemblage gently but firmly in your hand to support the tack fusing on the star.
6. Use your rosary pliers to bend over the tips of each star petal onto the top edge of the stone. Work from opposite directions, for example: north, east, south, west.
7. Use the chain pliers to adjust until the stone feels firm in the setting.
8. Tumble to harden and polish. Word of caution: Keep an eye on your stone to make sure it doesn't get damaged in the polishing process.

The tips of the five-pointed star are carefully bent.

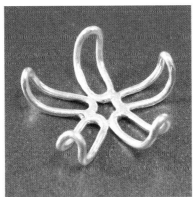

This back of the star remains flat and lies level.

Set the stone by assembling star and daisy beneath it, then closing the tips of the five-pointed star. When all are equal and holding the piece together with equal tension, squeeze the legs of the star together to create more compact effect.

A five-pointed star and five-pointed daisy are combined to create a beautiful gem setting.

Far left:
Be creative and explore variations on how to form the daisy and star. In this version, the star petals are squeezed narrow.

Left:
See what happens if you also curl up the daisy after the stone is set.

Hugs & Kisses

Passion Flower

When I was teaching drawing classes in the mid-1980s, I brought passion flowers in one day for our subject matter. My students were excited by the flower's intricate microcosm. By the end of the three-hour period, they were all about to have a nervous breakdown from trying to capture the details.

My favorite part about the Matchsticks & Torches and Hugs & Kisses Series is all the variations that you can come up with. The Passion Flower is a luscious combination of both.

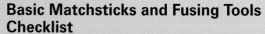

Basic Matchsticks and Fusing Tools Checklist

Use the basic setup for fusing and making matchsticks. Add/substitute the following:

- Dowel rod: 3/8 inch for small petals. Experiment with 1/2 inch for medium and 5/8 inch for large petals.
- Two needle-nose chain pliers

Basic Matchsticks and Fusing Materials Checklist

- 22-gauge (or thinner) wire to fit into the 10mm Swarovski hear crystal bead holes)
- 16-gauge fine silver
- 10mm Swarovski heart crystals (five per pendant)
- 14mm cabochons or Swarovski rivoli crystals

1. After tack fusing the star together, cut the ends of the rays open to create spokes.

2. Using the skills (and tools) for the matchstick projects, draw a bead at the end of each wire on the spoke.

3. Three silver components for Passion Flower.

4. The matchstick spoke is sandwiched between the star (bottom) and daisy (top) for a total of three layers. Set the stone the same way as with the lotus project to create the tension that holds the unit together.

To Add Crystal Petals to the Passion Flower

Whenever I teach in Hawaii, I am blown away by the beautiful and fragrant flowers that you encounter in your everyday routine. The bold colors (and color combinations) inevitably work their way into my jewelry projects, especially if I'm near bead stores and gemstones.

To add dimension to the passion flower, use Swarovski crystal hearts or any bead that is flat and triangular in shape. They easily wedge into the radial design from the side. Make a mini matchstick headpin to "sew" the hearts individually in place. The head pin should be thick enough to provide stability, while thin enough not to stress and break the bead hole edges. Fine silver is naturally soft, so it's easy to use in a "sewing" situation. Be sure to tuck in the ends of the wires so they don't snag or scratch.

Final Note: Traditional cabochons are flat backed and symmetrically round or oval in shape. Round ones work well in this design, and there aren't any special considerations in regard to tension setting. While rivolis have pointed bottoms that seat right into the daisy's center, cabochons are flat, so they might scoot around a bit more when you press down the star prongs. Experience is the teacher now, so have fun trying new ideas on this design.

Matchsticks and Torches

Pretty Prongs

I would like to leave you with two more ideas. After everything you've learned in this book, you will have the insight to create these. There aren't any new skills, just new ways of applying them. I hope they inspire you to forge out on your own and show us something we haven't seen before!

How the Pretty Prongs Were Made

The objects that I tend to choose for this style of prong setting are flat on the back to offer a platform for the piece to rest on. This helps stabilize the design. In particular, shells with corrugated/scalloped surfaces and edges give the matchstick prongs a trough to lie in or hold onto.

I used 16-gauge wire to frame/echo the back of the object's shape, then fused it closed. The prongs are double-headed matchsticks that have been bent into a U-shape. The center of the "U" was then aligned and fused onto the wire frame. A general prong length to begin working with is a 2-inch length after drawing the first bead.

To hang a visually complementary bead from the bottom of the pendant (while preventing stress on the frame or prongs), I sandwiched a vertical wire between the shell and frame, down the back.

The top of this wire ends in a coiled loop just big enough for the chain. I was also lucky enough to find a matching drilled donut bead and elongated pearl. Together, I was able to construct a matching toggle clasp. Visually, the piece is unified by materials (shell) and color (white). After I completed the piece I noticed that the matchstick prongs weren't stiff enough to grab the seashell securely, so I tumbled the pendant. At the time, I had no guarantee that the tumbler wouldn't damage the shell, but in the end, it actually cleaned up and polished the seashell quite nicely.

This system of harnessing found objects works well with coins, buttons, and sea glass. Shorten the prongs or curl them into spirals on the front to add variation and visual interest. If you have a somewhat boring object, make the metal the focal point of interest.

Whimsical Matchstick Creatures

I'm a firm believer in experimentation. When I was young, if a piece didn't go in the direction that I wanted, I would become frustrated, throw it away, and start over. Needless to say, I went nowhere very fast. As a mature artist, I've learned not to panic but to listen to my pieces and see which direction they want to go. Ironically, I never make mistakes anymore because everything has creative potential!

By enjoying the new pathways and adventures that my work directs me toward, I remain entertained and creative, and I learn new ways of working each day. These Whimsical Creatures were the results of a failed Pretty Prong project. I would never have deliberately set out to make such objects, but there they were one day, looking at me and asking me to help them stand up. By juxtaposing them with collections in my studio, I've given them a context (purpose) and helped you to "see" them too.

These fused fine silver worker bee assemblages were made from 16-gauge wire, tumbled and polished agates, sea shell, undrilled beads and cabochons.

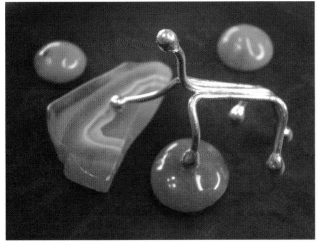

Conclusion

Ursula, Iris, and the Big Green Ring

What inspires you to make jewelry? Is it a piece that has been passed down through generations in your family? Is it something you've seen in a museum, created by a mysterious culture on the other side of the globe? Is it an event that you want to physically capture and imbue with zeitgeist? Below is a story of my earliest impression of a piece of jewelry told both through my mother and I.

The Ring

Emailed by my mother, Ursula, age seventy-three, December 8, 2008:

Let's see what I remember about "The Ring."

I was twenty-seven years old. I know it was my day off from work (NCO Club, Open Mess, Ramstein Air Force Base in Germany) because you were with me and all my days off were promised to you. I remember being in Landstuhl, crossing the Market Place Center to get to a store – the souvenir kind that has a lot of Fasching [Mardi Gras German style] type of jewelry. It was February and I planned to dress up as a gypsy, and that required a lot of chains with coins as it is typical for gypsy dress-up. I am not sure, but I think you were four years old. As we looked around, I did not like the jewelry they offered; I don't know if it was the jewelry or money or both. But when I saw The Ring, there were four of them: two in red and two in green. Two of them were oval and two squared (a red and green of each shape). The red one was gorgeous too but very "loud." All of them were stamped 1000. The store owner told me that they were handmade by an artist who was creating all kinds of jewelry for sale. I did not question his info. I really did not care 'cause I already was in love with it. I don't know what we did afterwards and if The Ring was the only thing I bought, but I am sure we had a wonderful time that day, as we always had on my days off.

Now the next thing I remember is showing it off and some guy said that The Ring would be even prettier in gold. Well, like a fool, I took it to a jeweler and had it gold plated. I was really upset when I saw the result. I mean they did a good job, but the only thing that came to my mind was *hideous*. I took it back to the same jeweler and asked them to take the gold off, but to preserve the 1000 stamp. As you can see the stamp was lost. I felt foolish enough as it was, so I did not go back. I was probably out of money at that point too.

Over the years, as fashion changed, The Ring suddenly became a great hit. It was called a "dinner ring" (or Pope- or Cardinal-Ring). It was worn on your right hand pointer finger. Also sometimes as a cocktail ring on top of a certain type of glove, on the same finger. No kidding. Just like the Pope. I also wore The Ring a lot selling real estate. It went so well with my Century 21 suit and Special Edition Jaguar. Ha ha ha.

I love you,
Mom

The Same Ring (My Story)

When I was a child, and when I had the opportunity (with or without permission), I would carefully look through my mother's jewelry boxes, which were always on her bedroom dressers or drawers. I would study all the individual pieces of earrings, necklaces, bracelets, and rings. The Green Ring was my favorite. It was so large that it reminded me of the kind of jewelry that had magical powers in fairytale books. The flawless teal stone was unusual because the color was so deep. It also complimented my mother's auburn hair and intense blue eyes. The patina made it seem ancient and exotic. I would occasionally be allowed to try the ring on under supervision. I would try it on several fingers, secretly assessing whether or not I had grown into it yet, hoping that someday, when it fit, she would give it to me. Sometime in my thirties, I gave up hoping and dropping hints, but I never stopped trying it on.

The Green Ring has been burned into my psyche since early childhood. It is magnificent, mysterious, and magical, but most of all, it became the icon that represented all the facets of my mother's difficult life journey.

My mother, who lives in coastal North Carolina, was not able to come to my fiftieth birthday because she had the rare opportunity to visit her brother in Munich. I was disappointed and she knew it. She sent a giant box instead and as I began opening it, I was puzzled to find cans of boiled peanuts, green beans, and corn with a note saying "for your pot-luck birthday party." It was a joke and we all had a big laugh. I continued to dig through the packaging to find the birthday card and found more boxes within boxes. Inside one it said, "I love you this much," written on a very long piece of paper. Then there was another box. The whole thing was very silly. I expected to find a check for some birthday money folded up, nice and neat, in the last, small box. Instead, when I opened a little fuzzy jewelry box, there it was: The Big Green Ring. I was stunned, and my eyes filled up with tears. When I called her later, all I could do was sob into the phone. Joy, mixed with an uneasiness that my mother, in her early seventies, was relinquishing her ring.

64